EMBRACE WHAT YOU DON'T KNOW

A Stupid Guide to Smart Business Leadership

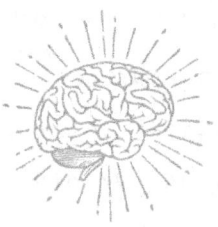

DAVID ACHATA

Published by Market Refined Publishing,
An Imprint of Market Refined Media, LLC
193 Cleo Circle
Ringgold GA 30736
marketrefinedmedia.com

Cover and Interior Design by Nelly Murariu at PixBeeDesign.com

Manuscript Edits by Ariel Curry and Market Refined Media

Print ISBN: 979-8-9855797-7-2
Digital ISBN: 979-8-9855797-8-9

Library of Congress Control Number: 2022914826

First Edition: November 2022

CONTENTS

FOREWORD

Several years ago, Wilson Lumber had a problem. As President of the company, I knew we had several managerial positions opening up, with no one in-house applying for them. As our company approached nearly seventy years, we had hit major growth, but our inability to develop leaders within the company was an issue we had to face. Why wasn't anyone taking these positions? Wasn't this a great place to work? What's wrong with these people? As so often is the case, the problem with "these people" was their leader. It's not an easy thing to admit, but I was the problem.

I heard about David Achata through the grapevine after he had worked with a local non-profit. I called him and asked if he would come in and coach our employees. What I found, however, was that I and the rest of our leadership team had our own growing to do.

To me, the solution seemed simple. Learn a little about how to encourage folks and remind them that they really did want to be a manager. Then presto! Our problems would be solved. At the time, we were bringing in around 65 million dollars in revenue with about 25 managers. Our growth dictated that we hire 15 more, and quickly.

As our team discussed these open positions (among other topics), remarks usually went like this: "People just don't want to work," or "All they care about is getting paid on Friday." I don't know, perhaps there's a grain of truth to that. But the harder truth was, we were just too busy to worry about what people actually needed from their leadership.

So, we brought David in to do some interviews with our staff. Though we initially thought that it might be a waste of time, these discussions proved to be incredibly helpful, revealing that our managers needed much more than simple coaching skills. They needed a framework for leading, as well as a genuine appreciation for people. More than that, they needed to know what the president of the company (that's me) and the executive leadership team expected of them.

What we created together has become sessions we call "Wilson Lumber Grows." In these sessions, our leaders learn how to develop trust through vulnerability and storytelling. They also discover their own personality and leadership style and how their past influences their present behavior. To create effective teams, we taught them how to develop people to their specific strengths and how to work together using those strengths.

The operating system beneath the success of Wilson Lumber Grows was learning to ask the right questions, or as David says, "embracing what you don't know." Great coaching is about helping get focused on the right goal and taking a question-asking journey to get to a resolution that makes sense. Getting this right has changed a lot for us.

As a result, each manager in our organization has learned to value those around them. The same teammates they used to complain about, they now see as a unique and important part of the business. Are we perfect? Of course not. But we've come a long way. Today, our management team numbers are in the mid-40s, and we've added more Wilson Lumber Grows sessions to accommodate them. Though we still have a few open management positions, we now have a process through which to train our own emerging leaders. This process has been an important factor that's led to our revenue surpassing well over 145 million dollars annually.

I was recently in a team meeting where the manager, previously known for his "do as I say" attitude, was humbly and persuasively soliciting feedback about how he and the company could improve. Maybe you know someone like him. He used to say things like, "I was raised where you just do as you're told, and that's what I expect." In this team meeting, however, something had shifted. I heard him say, "The reason your feedback is important, is that we really do care about you guys and want to make this a great place to work." By being open to discovering things about himself, he learned to appreciate and value the opinion of others. He's still improving, and as he gets better, the company does, too.

My belief is that growth and success in life are rooted in humility. You may not think so yet. Maybe you've bought into the lie that says success is about amassing wealth, security, and a grandiose reputation. However, it's been proven time and again that those things don't bring lasting contentment, much less happiness. I believe we find success when we embrace the humility to seek help, work on self-improvement, and accept ways we can change for the better.

At Wilson Lumber, we've often come across leaders that do not know their blind spots, their life stage, or even their leadership style—critical things that David explains within this book. But what we've seen over and over, is that if they're willing to learn, they'll grow and lead their respective teams toward success.

In the following pages, David describes how one's personal and organizational growth is dependent on the humility of the one(s) leading them—their willingness to ask questions and learn from those around them. This is what it means to embrace what you don't know. Who am I? How am I perceived by my team? In what areas do I need to grow? These are all questions that will lead to greater health, contentment, and joy, while reaping the financial benefits at the same time.

This book is about you and your growth as a person and as a leader. Read it, dwell on it, take it seriously, and humbly become the person and leader that you are meant to be.

Robb Wilson
Owner/President, Wilson Lumber Inc.
Madison, Alabama

PREFACE

I was born into chaos. My parents came from very different backgrounds, and they fought—a lot! Coming from different cultures, thousands of miles apart, they had different ways of doing things and their arguing only intensified the older I grew. The fallout from their relationship is something I'm still cleaning up today.

As an adult, I look back now and see more clearly how my origin story impacted me. As you'll see in a moment, no one who knew me when I was young would have imagined I'd grow up to do the kind of work I do now. My life was crazy—and everything I've built since then has been my way to find stability. This book is about the simple ways I've found steadiness and how I've helped many people and organizations do the same.

Today, working as a leadership coach and consultant, my heart is set on helping people and organizations find peace, purpose, and to flourish (items I'll address later on). I wrote this book to reflect on my story, synthesize what I know, and pass on the important lessons I've learned. My hope is that you'll reflect on your own story as you read mine, absorb the lessons, and use them to bring benefit to the places where you live and work.

The idea for this book came from a conversation with my daughter, Ana. One evening at the dinner table, she shared how she really wasn't sure how to describe the kind of work I do to her friends. "It's kind of like detective work," I said. "Companies usually have a pain point, like needing to train new leaders, or improving teamwork. Sometimes I honestly don't know what I'm going to learn when I go in to do an assessment. I ask a lot of questions, and see what themes rise to the top."

Ana chuckled and said, "Dad, your next book needs to be called 'How to Embrace Your Stupidity and Get Paid for It!'" We both died laughing thinking of how most people don't want to appear stupid, so they pretend to be smart. But the problem is that by doing that, they appear more foolish. "So what I do," I continued with Ana, "is help people get comfortable *asking* instead of telling. And by doing that, they find the answers they've been looking for."

I'm thankful for my daughter's observation. She knows that when I'm at my best, I'm a very curious person. Learning the art of question-asking helped activate my natural abilities and accelerate my career. But before I ever learned these skills, my worldview was forming as I watched my parents argue. To understand this book, you need to understand me. And to understand me, you need to know my story. So let's go back in time and start with my dad and mom, and how life with them sent me on a quest to find focus.

MY PARENTS

My father immigrated to America from Peru in the 1950s for college and was promptly drafted into the United States Army. He and another man were sent to Germany. The rest of his platoon went to Korea.

As a medic, he was stationed in the town of Baumholder where it wasn't uncommon to be jolted out of bed in the middle of the night and moved quickly to the Black Forest for military exercises.

"Why do you think they make us do this at 2:00 a.m.?" the men whispered.

Overhearing this one night, their Sergeant replied, "Do you think the Russians are going to care what time it is when they attack us?"

My father's young adult years were shaped under this cloud of impending doom. Things in the military were urgent, and he always had to be ready. He raised me this way, and I'm thankful for it. However, having a military man for a dad also brought its problems, which I'll share in a moment.

My mother was born in the small coal mining town of Big Stone Gap, next to Appalachia, Virginia. Her parents were teachers, and they were poor. She grew tired of moving every few years and taking care of her younger siblings. So, at fourteen, she left home on a train and paid her own way through boarding school, eventually becoming a nurse earning a master's degree in community health.

I grew up between conversations about the military and medical care—combat and war on one side, and outbreaks of diseases on the other. My parents bickered constantly, and as a child, I remember noticing what horrible listeners they were. Both had come from turbulent backgrounds, and that's what they recreated. Without knowing it, this was the environment that taught me the importance of hearing someone out. Even though I was young, I still understood that they were each fighting for peace, just in the wrong way.

FORMATIVE YEARS

While my mother was pregnant with me, she came home one day to our trailer vandalized. Other times, parked vehicles had been set on fire. One day, she came home and her dog had been shot. Break-ins occurred regularly, too, so she started carrying a gun. Over time, she discovered it was her ex-husband (who had bi-polar disorder) and he wasn't happy about her relationship with my dad. She got the law involved, and his retribution subsided.

When I was born, however, the turmoil continued. My dad had an anger problem, and my half-brother (from his first marriage) was over it. During an argument in the garage one evening, my brother tried to stab my dad with a broomstick. My dad dodged it and the broom-stick went through the garage door. A piece of utility tape was placed over the hole, and I grew up looking at it, wondering what had happened.

Research shows that the emotional development of a child while in-utero is impacted by the mother's emotional state. The fetus literally absorbs stress chemicals that can lead to depression, anxiety, ADHD, and a host of other issues when the child is born.[1] As you're about to see – I was impacted by the hostile environment I was formed in.

When I came of school age, it was discovered that I had dyslexia. The fact that my home lacked peace only added fuel to that flame. I couldn't concentrate, words and letters looked like fuzz to me, and everything I touched failed. Growing up, my mother spent more on tutors than the actual cost of private school. Yet even with her efforts, I barely graduated high school. Senior year, my GPA was 1.7.

"You do realize you won't be able to graduate with this number, right?" said the guidance counselor.

But I didn't care. My high school years were going up in a puff of smoke. I believed I was a failure, and a fail-ure fails. That's who they are and that's what they do. My life was a wreck and I felt there was nothing I could do about it. Until one day, that changed.

A few young men from the local Christian college came to work at my school and noticed me. They opened their lives and showed this frazzled teenager what healthy relationships looked like. They helped me find faith and purpose. I dropped my bad habits and began to see a brighter future. I'm deeply indebted to these men, without whom I might be dead. I'm so grateful I'm here—with you—today.

FINDING FOCUS

I buckled down and pulled my GPA up to a 2.3, barely graduating. My ambition for more educational torture was zero. "I don't think I want to go to college," I told my mother one day. "That's okay," she said, "But you'll need to move out and figure out what life is like on your own while you work a normal job. Life is hard with no education."

That was the motivation I needed to go to college. But what would I do? With little direction, I pondered the few things I knew for certain. My life had transformed, and I wanted that for others. Someone mentioned pastoral work to me once, so I went with that idea. I walked into the registrar's office at the local college and figured out how to enroll. My mom took a job there to get me a discount, and I worked three jobs to pay for the rest. I couldn't believe it—the thing I thought I'd never do, I was doing!

Upon beginning my classes, I noticed the strangest thing: My classmates were dropping courses left and right.

When I asked them why, they said that a subpar grade would negatively impact their entire grade point average, so they chose to drop the class all together.

But you'll never finish that way, I thought. *What's the good in avoiding the inevitable?*

Though I had a hard time in school as a child, my struggles taught me an important principle that's helped me find focus: Just don't quit! School was torture to me, but I knew that dropping classes now would only mean I have to take them again later. Why would I do anything to prolong it?

I was never very concerned with making good grades anyway, so they were inconsequential. I just wanted to acquire knowledge and become a better person. Without realizing it, I grew to embrace another focus principle: Learn what's important for you. I was determined to be happy in this life of mine.

Years later, my ability to engage scholastically improved. I entered my master's program courageously, but I encountered another obstacle. Those massive textbooks were filled with words I didn't understand. As I witnessed my classmates dropping more classes, I created another practice I still use today: Simplify.

Finding a thesaurus, I rewrote textbooks, putting the content into simpler terms that I could understand. This produced top grades in Greek, hermeneutics, and more. My friends noticed and asked for my notes. This led to yet another important life principle: Share what you know. After all, the one who teaches is the one who learns the most.

This holy trinity of principles—don't quit, simplify the important, and share it with others—helped me survive adolescence and find focus in young adulthood.

EARLY PROFESSIONAL YEARS

My philosophy aided me well as I learned leadership in a large church. Overseeing teams in a volunteer organization was how I discovered my knack for leadership development. During those years, we did important work and saw lives change for the better. But after about ten years of pastoring, a friend asked me a question that altered everything.

"Have you ever considered becoming a coach? I mean, you're kind of doing that right now in the church." She knew I wasn't satisfied where I was.

But what else was I fit for? After all, what good was a degree in Divinity in the "real world"? As we continued the conversation, she connected me with her husband, Sam, who had walked a similar path. Sam became one of my closest friends and colleagues and encouraged me to get some training and try my hand at coaching. That's exactly what I did.

EXPLORING THE UNKNOWN

My church was connected to one of the largest health care providers in central Florida, and I was surrounded by executives in the corporate space. As I received my coaching training, they allowed me to hone my skills on them. For the first time in my life, I found a profession that gave me the freedom to embrace what I didn't know. My whole life I'd struggled to overcome internal feelings of inadequacy, and though I'd found success as a leader, I still carried the nagging feeling that I was an imposter. Coaching taught me to get in touch with myself, my questions, and to be comfortable exploring what I didn't understand. I was good at it, and my executive friends encouraged and supported me as I retooled to start a new career. A few of those leaders eventually hired me, and that's when I took a leap of faith.

Sam had been talking about me and my new leadership associates, and a wealthy businessman from out of town overheard—a stranger who offered up his rental house for free as a first step in helping us get reestablished in my new profession.

"I don't know who these people are," he said, "but I feel as if I should help them."

That was the catalyst my family needed to plan for a fresh start. A few months later, we moved from Orlando, Florida, to Vancouver, Washington. We left everything—our home, our families, my career as a pastor—and started over. The housing market was upside down, too, so my wife (whom I had met in college) and I also lost $100,000 in equity when we short-sold our home. For us, that meant starting over financially—from ground zero.

I can say now, having nothing was a real motivator to make something happen. I don't recommend it as a strategy, but at the time, I felt it was what I had to do. It was hard, and I still bear the material and emotional scars from it today.

During that difficult time, an executive friend gave me some of the best advice I've ever received. "Say yes to everything," he nudged. "That way you'll learn quickly what you're good at and what you enjoy."

I followed his guidance, accepting that free rental and even living on food stamps for a while. I hammered out emails and wrote workshop material. I joined networking clubs and pitched my coaching services to anyone who was interested. I said yes to everything, and I grew immensely.

MY BIG BREAK

Then one day, lo and behold, a client responded to a bulk email I'd sent, asking how much I would charge to come do a workshop. When I gave him an estimate, he said my initial asking price was too low. To be taken seriously, I'd have to charge double the amount. That's how I found my way into the world of corporate work-shops and executive off-sites. Overnight, I went from food stamps to making thousands of dollars a day. I was humbled. I was honored. Could life get any better?

About six months later, I got another call from a well-known entrepreneur asking how much my fee would be for an organizational health assessment. His company had grown from two hundred to over six hundred employees in just a few years, and he wondered how healthy it was.

The two of us had met through a mutual acquaintance, months earlier, hit it off, and exchanged numbers. Now here he was, on the phone, asking me how to gauge the health of his company. Following the advice of my executive friend, I said, "I'd love to do that for you, but give me a few days to think about it."

It just so happened that I lived next to two consultants who worked for Microsoft. I didn't know the world of consulting yet, but I did understand how to ask the right questions. Armed with that, I asked my neighbors how I should go about it. They walked me through the consulting process, and I'm grateful to them. Suddenly, I went from a team of one to a team of three, and my paycheck skyrocketed. Only eighteen months after food stamps, I went from nothing, to running a full-on consulting agency. We were small, but we were powerful.

How did I get here so fast? I wondered.

From today's vantage point, I can say that my chaotic past wired me to do whatever necessary to find focus and create stability. Doing this for myself first helped me become a functional adult. Now I do this with my clients.

It's been over a decade since then, and I've learned a lot. It hasn't always been easy. In fact, I've endured my share of hardship. But in terms of personal growth, I've gained wisdom and industry knowledge that carries me on today. I know what I'm good at, and I focus there. But it didn't start that way. It started in the wild waters of turmoil.

YOUR STORY IS IMPORTANT

As a child, I didn't realize my circumstances were forming me into a certain kind of person. I've heard it said that we teach what we most need to know. Understanding that, it makes sense that I became a coach. And because of my personal experience, I work toward three goals:

1. To help leaders find peace

2. To use turmoil as a pathway to purpose

3. To help organizations bring healing to the world

Good leadership is the difference between flourishing or floundering, so I focus on leading. I grew up in chaos, and I decided that I was done with it. I exist now to bring peace and purpose to my home, the town where I live, and to my corporate work. Leadership isn't about creating chaos. It's about driving these right outcomes. I want you and your organization to get this, too.

You also have a story to tell fueled by your own life experience. Your past has hardwired you to say, "Hell no" to certain things, and "Heavens yes" to others. If you give yourself permission to pursue that train of thought—to discover the beauty that comes from what only you can create—your unique life will reveal a legacy you'll leave behind.[2]

This is only the beginning of my story, of our story. It's the operating system beneath everything you're about to read. This book is subtitled *A Stupid Guide to Smart Business Leadership* because a book can't change you—only time and practice can. But if I'm honest, there have been plenty of times that *I've* been stupid. I pretended I knew when I really didn't, and no one benefited. I want to save you from that and share some hard-learned lessons. It's my hope that as you spend time applying the principles in this book, you too can flourish in your life, leadership, and organization.

David Achata
Founder, The Achata Coaching & Leadership Group

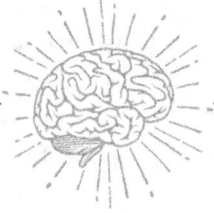

"If you want to improve, be content to be thought of as foolish and stupid."
— Epictetus

INTRODUCTION:
JOIN ME IN THE OFFICE

In my line of work, if I don't embrace what I don't know, I don't get paid. What you're about to read is a conversation I have with clients on a regular basis.

It was a sunny day in Orange County, California. I'd been called in to interview members of an executive team at a large technology company in preparation to lead a strategy session.

"What's your education, your background?" the General Manager asked me from behind his desk.

Now, most people might answer with their credentials or experience. But I'm not most people. I'm an expert at not being an expert. Honestly, I didn't know why he was asking that question. So I did what you do when you're in touch with what you don't know. I asked him about it.

"Why are you asking?" I replied.

"Well," he said, "if I'm going to hire someone to tell my team what to do, I need to know what kind of experience they have."

Ahhh, I thought. *This man thinks I'm a business consultant.*

"Oh, I'm actually not here to tell your team what to do," I replied. "I'm here as a coach, which is a Thinking

Partner. I'm a trained question-asker. A coach draws out information that only the client knows, to help clarify and gain movement on their goals. You are the only expert on you."

"Oh," he said (a little confused). "How is that helpful to me?"

"The higher you go in any organization, the less likely people are to tell you the truth," I replied (and he nodded his head in agreement). I continued, "In fact, I'm probably one of the few people who will admit when I don't understand what you're talking about. A lot of people won't confess they're not tracking what's being said because they don't want to appear stupid. I, on the other hand, am trained to slow you down, to ask you questions, and help you think (and communicate) more clearly. I'll do that for your team, too. Do you see how that could that be valuable for you?"

Though he didn't answer directly, he agreed. "Oh," he exclaimed, "that makes a lot of sense. I like it," he said. "You're hired."

Believe it or not, that conversation opened the door to over a half-million dollars' worth of work.

THE TOP LEADERSHIP TRAIT

People get into leadership for different reasons. Some get into it for the power. Others are pulled into it circumstantially. But when leaders are at their best, they do it out of a sense of responsibility for others and to a higher cause.

A study of three-hundred thousand business leaders revealed that the top trait needed in a leader is the ability to inspire and motivate.[3] At his core, that manager in Orange County knew that if he was going to lead people well, he needed help with his blind spots because the areas where we don't see our pitfalls are the areas that will derail everything.

Leadership guru Peter Drucker noted how we are overconfident in leaders with natural abilities to inspire others. From his observation, the best leaders are actually self-made. "We need far too many leaders to depend only on the naturals," he said. Leadership isn't just a magnetic personality, or salesmanship. It's "the lifting of a man's vision to higher sights, the raising of a man's performance to a higher standard, the building of a man's personality beyond its normal limitations."[4] Drucker knew that we all have limitations. Therefore, to go farther, we need outside help learning to embrace what we don't yet know if we're going to do our best work.

It's a noble undertaking to lift people's vision to higher sights — and I want to call you to it. Why did you get into leadership? What are you working toward? I got into it because I wanted to see lives changed for the better. But, as I mentioned earlier, I was afraid of being seen as an imposter. The man behind the desk in Orange County knew he had a responsibility to think and communicate clearly. He was responsible to his business, and the cause for which they worked. But in his insecurity, right out of the gate, he asked for my credentials.

WE MOSTLY HAVE THE SAME FEAR

I've learned through the years that many of my clients mask their insecurity with loud voices, fast-paced schedules, and comparing themselves against one another while swapping qualifications and accomplishments. It's all a cover up for the fear of it being discovered that they don't actually know everything.

Imposter Syndrome is the top fear of leaders,[5] and I can confirm that many of my executive clients would agree. *People will discover that I don't know what I'm doing,* they think. So somewhere along the way, we stop asking questions, and we start telling. Like the man in the office in Orange County, we're conditioned to value credentials, not relationship building or understanding. We exchange data, assuming we understand one another. Even worse, when it comes to inspiring and motivating, we think if we puff out our chests and talk louder, it will make people want to follow.

If you've ever tried to lead a classroom of children, you'll know that talking louder only escalates the disorder. You've actually got to talk quieter. It's not uncommon for a client to meet me for a session and say, "Can we do this in fifteen minutes? I've got so many urgent things to do, I need to cut this session short."

"You sound really busy," I respond. "Would it be okay if we spent a few minutes in silence?" When I slow them down, they often respond, "That's the quietest I've been in years." And once slowed down, they realize how much more time is needed to address the unknowns they're carrying around.

Going slower is what most people need. But it's the fear of looking stupid that keeps most people moving so fast. I try to embrace what I don't understand every day. I truly don't know why my clients are in a hurry. I have a lot of assumptions about their pace, but I don't know for sure. Sometimes they don't either, so I slow them down.

That man in Orange County didn't need another guy with more credentials. He needed someone with the right questions. I'm glad I questioned him about his questions. By embracing what I didn't understand, it enabled the two of us to walk a humble path (together) toward discovery, and we both benefited.

THE COST OF INSECURITY

Through the years, I've had multiple versions of this conversation before I'm hired. People are used to living in a world of information–exchange. They want quick fixes and sound bites they think will spawn speedy results. But commonly, growth isn't quick. It's slow, and when you're in the middle of it, it can feel painful. Maybe even a little awkward. The coaching part of my work is trying to get people used to embracing what they don't know because that's how we identify a part of the problem in order to make tangible progress on something that matters.

I walk this path all the time as I help people explore their lives, their leadership, and improve their organizations. Most people crave to be heard. And when that happens, even if the ideas we create aren't theirs specifically, they'll buy–in.

Professor Emeritus at the MIT Sloan School of Management, Edgar Schein, shares that one of the chief tasks of a helping professional (coach or consultant) is to help the client be comfortable asking questions or admitting what their actual worries are.[6] I would add that this needs to be one of the chief aims of leadership as well. As a friend from the past told me, "Together, we're a genius." Tapping into our collective knowledge is impossible without admitting what we don't know. Building from that point is how we do our best work. We've got to get away from our fear being seen as "not knowing."

Many of the disasters of our time could have been prevented if a healthier chain of communication existed. In 1986, the Challenger explosion was reduced to a faulty O-ring that engineers knew couldn't be used in cold temperatures.[7] Why didn't they speak up?

In 2005, it was discovered that the U.S. government knew a full day in advance that Hurricane Katrina would decimate the levees that protected New Orleans and cost 10 billion dollars just in the first week of devastation.[8] This isn't to mention that the U.S. Army Corps of Engineers only designed those walls to protect up to a category two or three storm. Since Katrina was a category four storm, why weren't those worried speaking up or acting? Why wasn't a better wall built in the first place? Why didn't leaders evacuate the city?

Maybe it's because we're such hopeful creatures that we don't act when we know better. But maybe it's rooted in us that we don't want to be seen as wrong if our worries don't come to fruition. *I'll be seen as incompetent,* we think. So we don't speak up. Our fear of looking inept comes out in the way we handle conflict, too.

In organizations, managers spend about 20% of their time dealing with conflict.[9] And what is conflict? It's what happens when two people can't talk about the same thing at the same time. Party A wants to talk about a harmful decision while Party B wants to talk about how they felt when spoken to the wrong way — two different subjects. It's hard to pause one's own agenda to understand what someone else is saying. It requires a comfort with the vulnerability of not knowing what the other party will say. Organizationally, you do the math. Think of how much you pay your managers and other leaders. Combine all those salaries and take out 20%. That's the chunk of your revenue you are losing every year because people are afraid of looking incompetent, or like they don't fully understand something.[10] The anxiety this creates in a workplace impacts individuals, too, who are each carrying around their own personal issues.

Adverse Childhood Experiences, or ACEs, are the potentially traumatic events that occur in our lives before we're 17 years old—and they leave a lasting mark on the people in your organization. "61% of adults surveyed across 25 states reported that they had experienced at least one type of ACE before age 18, and nearly 1 in 6 reported they had experienced four or more types of ACEs."[11] That means that about six out of 10 of the people who work in your organization are carrying around (or ignoring) the baggage of experiencing violence or neglect, suicide, substance abuse problems, mental health issues, or the pain of the instability created when their parents were separated or sent to jail or prison. It's no wonder managers spend 20% of their time addressing interpersonal conflict. People have no training and are carrying around a whirlwind of emotions that no one is asking about. This impacts the important work we're trying to do, and it affects our bottom line.

MY FRAMEWORK

This is why I created a simple framework to bring stability in the lives of my clients. It addresses the most basic categorical blind spots I've seen over and over. Here it is:

- ✔ In Life – know what life stage you're at so you can own your personal work.

- ✔ In Leadership – know your leadership style and how to get results through a team that owns issues.

- ✔ In Your Organization – know your Noble Cause[12] and how to address what could stop you.

Life is crazy enough. It's up to you as a leader to help bring stability in these places so people's energy can be freed up to address the other things they're dealing with along the way. My framework doesn't address everything, but it addresses the basic things to help people find stability and flourish.

THREE AREAS WE'LL EXPLORE

Even the smartest people and organizations are ignorant at times. That *isn't* stupid. Stupidity is knowing you don't have the answer and acting as if you do. I want to save you from that in your life, leadership, and organization.

Do you (or those you lead) need to find focus and meaning in life? Are you ready to discover better ways of operating and leading at work? Is your organization ready for a tune-up? If you resonate with any (or all) of these questions, this framework is for you. You've come to the right place. I'm here to help you find the answers.

Success comes when you allow yourself to "own" what you don't know, and that puts you ahead of the game. If, by chance, you're someone who thinks you'll just figure things out with time (like I used to), I want to help you avoid a few common pitfalls and accelerate your success. But for those ready to admit you need some help, think about reaching out to a trained coach or trusted guide (apart from reading this book). If that sounds like something you would be open to, see my contact information at the conclusion of the final chapter. Be patient, though; this simple yet informative read covers several of the difficulties experienced within leadership positions in almost every kind of work.

WHO THIS BOOK IS FOR

I wrote this book for leaders like me. Maybe you came from an unstructured or chaotic background, and you had to figure things out yourself. Or perhaps you took up the mantle of responsibility before you should have. Sure, this helped you survive, but it also put you in charge of everything before you were ready. Now you're leading a team or organization and your sense of responsibility may be taking you fast toward the end of your limits. This book will help you with some basic principles to bring stability in your life, and in the lives of those you lead. But the starting place for all of it is learning to embrace what you may not know.

When you're finished, please pass along this resource to those people you think might benefit from it. Anyone can apply its lessons, though it was written primarily for those who lead from within a company (though the kind of businesses may vary widely).

MY WORK

In my career as a leadership coach, I work with brilliant people in a variety of industries such as technology, medicine, property development, manufacturing, and more. In these arenas, I'm approached by those looking for help in one or more of the following areas:

1. Leadership Coaching and Executive Health

2. Team and Strategy Development

3. Organizational Health and Leadership Training Programs

On the surface, these topics appear complex. But underneath, I always find human beings who are stuck and want to make forward momentum a priority when they see a path that aligns with their values and their company. I love my work because most people come eager to grow, and because it's fun to be a part of that process.

I've seen many wonderful things happen that seem to hinge on a few basic awareness points. In each section of this book, you'll read about life, leadership, and how your organization may pursue and achieve those points in abundance. This is followed by some questions and practical ways you can embrace what you don't know for the greater good. I'll share success stories along the way, too. In every one of those instances, the formula was simple—first, someone embraced what they didn't know, followed by the humility to ask the right questions, then applied the wisdom gained, and got paid for it. But payment is about more than money.

WHAT'S AHEAD

Financial goals are important, but they're not always controllable. They are indicators of success, but in themselves, they don't necessarily equate a positive outcome. Below, you'll find again a simple outline of this book, and how success is framed within it.

1. In life—I know the purpose of my life "stage" while creating healthy relationships and work to match.

2. In leadership—I know my style and get results through a team as they take greater ownership of issues.

3. In organizations—stakeholders know their Noble Cause and are motivated every day to work toward that vision.

When these definitions of success are at play, financial progress nearly always follows.

So technically, real payment does result. But the kind of payment I want you to achieve is deeper. It is possible to be financially wealthy and also to be miserable. That is NOT my wish for you.

A SUCCESS STORY

A struggling doctor in my community told me once, "I'd give all the money in the world to have what you have. You've got a healthy marriage, kids that want to be around you, and you're doing meaningful work in the world." Though Dr. Bill Jones (so called to guard his true identity) was financially well off, he was incredibly poor—emotionally speaking. Having gone through multiple divorces and lost custody of his children, he had still managed to build a successful business. But even that was beginning to fray. Employees were quitting in droves, and it was all he could do to keep his medical office staffed.

The thing is, Dr. Jones had no purpose in life. He had a controlling personality, and his staff members were afraid of him. What could he do? Exactly what I'm telling you now. He embraced what he didn't know, got humble by asking the right questions, learned from the answers (painful as the answers might have been), and got paid.

His personal transformation trickled down into the other parts of this life. He found a vision, restored his relationships with his kids, and changed the culture of his workplace. Now he's not just financially stable, relationally he's in a great place with a thriving practice and happy employees. I'll share more about his story in the book's conclusion, and I hope by then, you can add your success story to his.

Getting paid brings so much more than money. Getting paid means greater physical health, mental calm, and personal leadership that makes a human difference. This feeds into a growing organization and yields greater results that benefit everyone. Do you want that? If you're still reading, I'll assume that's a "Yes, please." Congratulations! You've taken the first step to embracing what you don't know.

When you admit what you don't know, you humanize yourself, thus connecting in a more meaningful way with others. You tap into a collective expedition that brings stronger bonds, driving the forward motion of everyone to succeed. Admitting what you don't know doesn't mean you aren't decisive. It means you're humble. People trust leaders like that. That's my goal for you!

PRINCIPLES WE'LL APPLY

As we launch into each section, I want to outline a few success principles. These statements will repeat throughout this book. Following each statement, you'll find its corresponding meaning.

1. **To embrace what you don't know** means—
   to acknowledge what you may be missing.

2. **To get humble by asking questions** means—
   to be vulnerable in order to find the help needed
   to do the work required. In short, to be willing
   to change.

3. **Get paid** means—to reap the benefits of your
   transformation.

The fundamental message of this book is found in these simple but rich details. To outwardly acknowledge to yourself what you may be missing—in your life, your leadership, and your organization. From there, I'll provide questions that will require a truthful answer. Your transparency will help decide how to integrate what you learn, and that will determine how you get paid. It's up to you.

SUMMARY

Embrace what you don't know

Trying to look smart when you don't completely understand is stupid. If you're wondering why someone is asking or telling you something, inquire. "Help me understand..." is one of the best ways to embrace what you don't know.

Get humble by asking the right questions

Are you someone who explores deeper when things are unclear? Or do you assume you know, talk louder, and try to sound more authoritative than you actually are? Another way to look at it: Do you question the questions? What's it costing you right now to overlook areas in your life or leadership where there's ambiguity? The way you know that you're in ambiguity is that you're carrying questions and resentment for things that aren't as you wish. Get curious about that.

Get paid

If you're a coach or consultant, or in a leadership role, seeking a greater understanding of what you don't know about your position (or ideas) will reward you with success, clarity and (most likely) real money eventually.

APPLICATION

What chapter points do I need to remember right now?

_____

_____

_____

_____

_____

_____

How do I want to make movement in these areas?

_____

_____

_____

_____

_____

_____

_____

When will I do it?

....

....

....

....

....

....

....

....

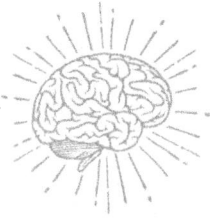

"There is such a great fire in one's soul, and yet nobody ever comes to warm themselves there, and passersby see nothing but a little smoke coming from the top of the chimney, and go on their way."

—Vincent van Gogh

Chapter 1

CREATING STABILITY AT EVERY STAGE OF LIFE

Have you ever been around a leader you knew wasn't doing their own personal work? They're easy to spot because their problems are always "out there." Since personal ownership is absent, they write people off and villainize them when approached with concerns. "It's not my fault," is the telltale response, and it comes out in many forms.

One of the most famous lines that illustrates this dynamic came on November 17, 1973, when Richard Nixon claimed, "I am not a crook" when challenged about his role in the Watergate Scandal.[13] It's common knowledge that Nixon recorded nearly every phone conversation and obsessed about what was going on in the outside world, as it related to his presidency. But in his attention to the external world, he was unable to acknowledge his internal issues.

In 2001, the Enron Corporation was involved in massive accounting fraud that led to a $74 billion loss for its shareholders. To which the founder stated in an interview for 60 minutes, "I don't think I'm a fool, but I think I was fooled... I can't take responsibility for the criminal conduct of someone inside the company."[14] Again, the problem was with "someone else."

After the May 2022 mass shooting at an elementary school in Texas, an NRA board member was questioned about the NRA's responsibility. "I'm not the one who pulled the trigger," he said.[15]

Of course, these are extreme examples. But each of these instances had an origin that was small. For those of us who are married or have children, what we know is that the smaller issues we had earlier in our marriage usually grow up to become bigger issues later on. With children, it's the same. What we notice as a potential problem in their character or development when they are small tends to grow up with them.

My point here is that when people aren't accustomed to looking inward, they turn into a particular kind of person—one who doesn't own problems (or who hasn't learned how to). These people certainly can't admit when they don't know something. With leaders, this creates a culture where no one else owns issues, either. This perpetuates a palpable instability in our lives, in the ways we lead, and in our organizations.

Sigmund Freud saw leadership denial as "a state of rational apprehension that does not result in appropriate action."[16] In other words, when confronted with a concern, a leader's personal anxiety can prevent them from saying and doing the appropriate things. How can this be fixed? Like most things, we get better with practice. And there's no better arena for practice than your own personal life. Therefore, it's important to know what life stage you're in because each developmental stage requires a particular kind of personal work that goes with it. So let's take a few moments to look inward.

The health of one's childhood and adolescence impacts how we mature. And if you're like me, you may still be cleaning up the shrapnel of events you encountered when you were young. As a child, I encountered learning struggles in school, bullying, and racism. Often, I felt I could not bring these things up at home due to the consistent arguing between my parents. And as we'll see in a moment (in the life stages), when a child is in survival mode before the age of six, they aren't able to look inward since their energy is spent on monitoring the outside world for danger.

I've given you a small window into my personal work, and I hope that, as you read, you will also see your own internal areas of need. From my experience, many of my clients are also like me. No matter the age, they still carry with them the scars from their own development and the shame that comes with that pain. And when shame comes in, it often goes the wrong direction, turns toxic, and attacks our core.

SHAME AND TOXIC SHAME

Recently, I took center stage to share a presentation during a personal intensive where I was dealing with some difficult parts of my past. Throughout the week, people began to joke about how smooth I was. I get this a lot, and its origins are in my chaotic past. It's my own coping mechanism—appear to be superman, that way no one can get close.

The mood was light in the room that day and someone made a comment about me being "Rico Suave." The facilitator (who was half Iranian) stopped the group and said in a kind tone, "that's racist." The group went silent for a moment, then a response came from the small crowd, "I'm not racist!" The facilitator responded calmly, "I never said you were racist, I said your comment was racist."

This interaction showcases one of the main problems people face when owning their own issues. They take something outside of themselves and make it an identity. When a blind spot is pointed out ("That's racist"), an individual will mount a defense against an internal and toxic thought that feels like a personal indictment at their core ("*I'm* not a racist"). This is a toxic, shame-based response. Though we'll unpack that last sentence in a moment, first, we must look at what shame is.

Consultant and counselor Chip Dodd writes, "Shame is the feeling that first brings us into relationship with ourselves because it makes us conscious of our incompleteness... shame tells us that we will always be people who are capable of harming others and failing."[17] Another way to think about this is that shame is a built-in mechanism we each possess that shows us that there's always more work to do personally and in our relationships.

Brené Brown has said, "Shame is the fear of disconnection [and that] I've not done something worthy of connection." She continues that "shame is the intensely painful experience of believing that we are flawed and therefore unworthy of love, belonging, and connection... shame is real pain.[18] That's when shame becomes toxic, and when problems happen.

Remember, "Together we're a genius" (from earlier)? It takes a lot of shame to get to that point on a team, or in any relationship. Shame is one mechanism (if felt rightly) that causes us to lean in and apologize when we've overstepped our bounds, or not done a job correctly. Psychologically speaking, when we say we're sorry and add personal narrative (stories), trust is formed, and attachments are made between people.[19]

Our culture is somewhat confused here. Accountability is healthy, yet it is often confused with shaming. Accountability is when we try to steer someone back on course. If shame is felt rightly, we will think; *Oh, I've made a mistake I need to fix.* However, accountability can turn into toxic shaming when people are called names, blame is shifted, and colleagues are treated as if their actions are synonymous with their self-worth. This is the breeding ground for people's greatest relational fear—disconnection.

To debate whether shame is good or bad misses the point. Judging our feelings can misguide us from embracing what we don't know. Since our feelings are real, we need to get curious and wonder what messages they are sending us.

Dodd continues that "impaired shame comes from our pasts. We have learned for survival's sake to hide, reject, or minimize our hearts... Toxic shame helps us so deny our natural condition that we are left with anxiety (dread of what will happen) and... we reject our natural call to seek help, reach for others, and expose our true giftedness... Toxic shame tells us that if we show our true selves, we will be rejected."[20] This is the real reason leaders deny responsibility, continue in ignorance and don't ask questions. We're just protecting ourselves from potential elimination.

What can be done? I believe that when we each look inward and work on the issues appropriate to the stage we're in, we can minimize toxic shame, find humility, and develop healthy relationships. Not doing this results in putting up a façade that everyone but us can see.

TOXIC SHAME: TWO EXAMPLES

Years ago, I was at an event and met Rick, who had recently completed an MBA. He looked young to me and over the course of the conversation I discovered he was only twenty-three. Rick had big dreams and shared with me how he was trying to get investors to give him a few million dollars in venture capital to create a product that was going to help save people in third world countries. No one would give him the money.

Rick had never worked a job as an adult, had no girlfriend, and still lived with his mom. One year later, Rick gave up on his idea and went back to school to get a different degree and another job. Rick was an adolescent in a man's body. He was full of ambition to do something good but lacked the humility that only comes with age. He was aiming to be at another stage of life before he was ready. Why? To be honest, I don't completely know. But I can guess his over-ambition was a coverup for some form of toxic shame. Somewhere in his past, he may have heard or believed he was a nobody. So he tried too hard to be someone at another stage in life. This happens with older people, too.

Recently, I stood in line for the restroom with my son at a wedding reception. Many of my business colleagues were there, and my family had joined me for the event. It was a wonderful night with amazing drinks, good music, and dancing. A few of the guys there (mostly in their 20s) had too much to drink and anxiously awaited their turn to relieve themselves. In burst an older man in his sixties. He pulled from his pocket a roll of hundred-dollar bills and started cutting the line while shoving money into the pockets of everyone in front of him as he laughed and talked about how bad he had to pee. My son, who was only twelve at the time, said to me afterward, "I wish I'd been in that line!" This made me sad, because I knew that man had once led a large and powerful company. I wished my son could have received a different lesson from an older man who had once held so much influence.

Though I don't know what led to a man in his mid-60s to behave this way, what I do know is that he was behaving like a teenager. Why? I wonder if, at some point in his past, he didn't have money, or was an outsider longing to be on the inside. He'd spent a lifetime running away from that feeling, and he was still doing it with a beer in his hand and a wad of hundred-dollar bills as he paid his way to the front.

What both of these examples have in common is that a lack of personal work resulted in major blind spots. My hope for everyone (these men, and you, and me) is that we'll all become the kind of people who face our issues, and by doing so, others will see they can face theirs, too. At every stage of life, there's work to do, and doing that work gives us practice at owning our stuff.

THE FIRST FIVE LIFE STAGES: AN OVERVIEW

It's important to know where you're at in life so you'll be able to put your focus in the right direction. Therefore, knowing your life "stage" and its corresponding work is of utmost importance.

The psychologist Erik Erikson believed there were eight stages of human development. Each is marked by an internal conflict, important events, and outcomes. He mapped these out in broad terms, and each stage is built on the previous one. Since we're embracing what we don't know, let's figure out what we may be missing considering our age and life stage. We won't cover all the stages here in detail, but I do want to give an overview of the first five, which are about childhood and adolescent development. After the first five, we'll dig into the latter stages of adulthood in detail.

- ✔ **Stage One:** Infancy — A baby learns to trust or mistrust the world.

- ✔ **Stage Two:** Toddlerhood — The timeframe where a 1- to 2-year-old learns if it's okay to be autonomous. Parental connection is important here because our parents help us develop our own will, or we develop shame based on how well we learned to clothe ourselves or use the bathroom.

✔ **Stage Three:** Early Childhood (ages 3 through 6) is the timeframe when a child learns to take initiative and find a sense of purpose.

✔ **Stage Four:** Middle childhood takes place between ages 7 and 10 as the child learns if they can make it in the world of people. The question, "What am I good at?" gets answered here. This stage is about competence.

✔ **Stage Five**: Adolescence happens between 11 and 19 and is when one finds an identity vs. the role confusion that can come in the earlier stages that weren't healthy. "Who am I?" and "Who can I be?" are the two important questions being asked in this stage.[21]

Understanding these stages is essential for leaders. If you weren't parented well, or endured a hardship of some sort, it may have stunted your emotional development. None of us has a perfect past, so at some point in life, we'll need to go back and face the toxic shame that can come with that. If you're someone who says, "I honestly can't locate a single problem with my upbringing," that response in itself reveals a potential blind spot.

Somewhere in mid-life, we must make a return and face issues that happened in childhood. What's more, our teams are full of people who might have the same set issues we have (and their own unique ones). As I've said repeatedly up to this point—when we can own our own issues and our past hurts, others can see how to do it, too. Looking inward will help you change for the better, and when you change for the better, the way you interact with the outside world will change, too.

As we dig deeper into the later stages of development, be curious. Where are you at? What about the members of your team? Now let's focus in detail on the adult stages of six and seven, followed by a brief word on stage eight.

STAGE SIX: INTIMACY VS. ISOLATION

The big question people ask between the ages of 19 and 40 is how close they should allow themselves to get to others. The important events in this stage involve finding the right relationships. Those who handle this stage well learn to love and to be loved. However, if a person is unable to navigate this stage correctly, it can lead to isolation (both in and beyond this stage).

An obstacle at stage six can occur for those who come out of their adolescent years (stages four and five) with an unclear sense of self. This leads to a hyper focus on one's competencies or achievements. To set goals and achieve them is fine, but not at the expense of one's relationships.

Sadly, those who try to find identity in their work or other accomplishments are found grasping at stage six. They may have accrued a nice bank account or an executive title, but they're lonely, they easily cut ties with relationships, or they drive others away. Can you think of a teammate like that? It could be a sign that their development in stage six was incomplete.

Leaders who are stuck in stage six have built up a life of success based on what they do—not who they are. They behave as if they're self-sufficient and therefore neglect to connect with others. And let's face it, humans need each other. Identity is not based on what we do. It is who we are apart from our accomplishments. If you don't get this right early on, then it's difficult to mature properly. Even more, you can't succeed professionally without relying on others. And even if you do, it will never be what it could have been if you'd built close relationships and a team to partner with. Therefore, the ability to navigate healthy connection with others is essential.

Those who have a clear sense of who they are find freedom to engage relationally. When one is clear on their feelings, then they can be clear on the thoughts that accompany those feelings.[22] Those things together form a unique voice, and using your voice is incredibly freeing. It's hard to have health in relationships without a voice, and if a leader doesn't use her voice, then she forms actions based on what others think and expect. This runs the potential of reactivity and, at some point, could cease to be leadership. Have you been doing that as a leader? If so, the good news is that you *can* heal up.

But you'll have to go back and face some of the earlier stuff that took your voice. This will slow you down, but I can almost guarantee, those around you will breathe a sigh of relief when you start looking inward.

Personally, I'm just starting to learn some of the particulars of using my voice. For years, I thought my voice was tied up in my faith, my personality, or the tangibles of my work. But I'm only now coming to accept the particulars of my story. One example is growing up bi-racial in east Tennessee. As a leader, I've noticed that when I share these parts of my story in the right setting, people lean in. Sometimes they disagree, yet even with disagreement, I've learned that when I share specifics of my experience, nearly always people say, "Aha, now I see what you're trying to say."

Though, age-wise, I'm beyond stage six, I'm going back in my story and experiencing vulnerability in new ways. This primarily comes out as I speak to the real events I lived through that harmed me with a counselor or trusted friends. As I face the real feelings and thoughts I have about those events, it helps me better navigate the world I live in now. Vulnerability is the antidote to shame. It's how we learn to overcome disconnection and use our voice.

At stage six we find our spouse, our closest friends, and the network that may be with us for the rest of our lives. Stage sixers ask: Who can I trust? Who do I want to journey with?

The work of Brené Brown is big for those in this stage. As a researcher, she found that vulnerability is the pathway toward relationship building and innovation.[23] Vulnerability is when we can admit when we don't have all the answers and solicit help from those around us. In the cases where we do have the answers, we pause to allow others a chance to contribute. This kind of behavior exhibits strength and creates confidence in teams. Environments like this bring decisiveness. The team leader has it, each player has it, and an atmosphere of safety is felt by all. In this space, expressing feelings of happiness, hurt, or embarrassment draws in the team to create, grow better, and get things done. It works the same in familial and other relational spaces. Create an ecosystem of safety and openness, and you'll reap the benefits.

If you're at stage six, embracing what you don't know is about discovering what a meaningful relationship is as you learn to use your voice. The benefit is learning to love and be loved. Some don't address stage six stuff until later in life, and that's okay. A wise man once said to me, "You're exactly where you're supposed to be." And so I say to you, don't rush it. When you're ready, you're ready. But I offer this caution: You will find yourself stuck at this stage if you fixate on yourself. You must find ways to connect to others by being vulnerable and using your voice.

Toxic shame shows up at stage six in the form of unhealthy self-sufficiency. Why? Leaders have a huge fear of being seen as needy by others. Healthy stage sixers aren't ruled by that fear. They have a good network of friends and colleagues that would carry their casket one day.

Stage Six Key Questions:

1. Who can I trust?

2. What's broken that's preventing me from being vulnerable with others?

3. How can I get help to address my internal deficits?

4. Who are those I can imagine journeying with for the long-haul? How will I make time for those relationships?

STAGE SEVEN: GENERATIVITY VS. STAGNATION

The big question people 40 to 65 tend to ask is *what (or who) will be my legacy*? In other words, what will they leave behind? The important events of this stage are work and parenthood. A successful outcome at this age is learning how to receive and give care. Failing at this stage can result in more self-absorption and stagnation of growth.

As we get older, it's natural to want something to outlast us, so we begin to question what the conclusion of our life will look like—what are we working towards? Sometimes, younger people in their thirties start thinking about this, and that's good. The problem is, if you haven't yet learned to navigate relationships in a healthy way (stage six), then you're creating something that may lack relational texture to leave behind for others.

This is the reason why it's difficult to stay in some workplaces as we age. If the culture was created by someone at a younger stage, as we mature, the company sometimes doesn't. We must either help it to grow or leave it. Those at stage seven should reach the point where they understand that life has become too important to mess around. So they buckle down and get focused on their most important relationships and/or what their contribution will be to the world. If their workplace helps in that effort, great. If not, they move on to a more mature work environment.

Erikson's stage seven is also about parenting. After all, those closest to you are the people you'll influence the most. Sure, you want to do meaningful work and impact others. But losing sight of those in your own home leads to regret.

Here's a question for you: Have you drawn boundaries and made a plan for how you'll invest in your family? Doing so will help you live and lead from a good place. A function of maturity is showing those coming up behind you how to live. Take your family seriously. Invest your energy there to impact the next generation. And as you do this, those you lead will see how to do it, too.

I'm currently in my mid-forties and preparing my daughter to go away for college. It's sobering to know my time with her is limited, and my son is close behind. Sure, I've got to work a job and pay my bills. But my personal work, and my best energy, needs to go toward my kids and marriage.

I've got several personalized trips planned with each of my children based on where they're at in life. I'm taking my 18-year-old daughter to different parts of the country to tour universities and meet strong women leaders and entrepreneurs. I recently took my 14-year-old son away for a weekend to talk about growing into a man of character. I have focused times with my wife, too, where we have fun (taking walks, date nights, or afternoon lunches) and work on our relationship (we see a counselor regularly, even when it's not a crisis). After all, my kids need to see their parents in a healthy relationship so they'll know how to do it one day.

If you're at stage seven, embracing what you don't know is about getting clear on where the health of your family may need some extra attention (if that's part of your life plan) and on accomplishing meaningful work. Don't get stuck thinking about one over the other. Consider both. The benefit you'll gain is clarity regarding your life's work and investing in the next generation.

Stage Seven Key Questions:

1. What (or who) will be my legacy?

2. How will my life count?

3. What will I pass on to the next generation?

A BRIEF WORD ON STAGE EIGHT

Around 65 years of age is when we begin to reflect on our lives; what we've accomplished and still need to do. If you're proud of what you've done, you'll feel a sense of integrity and satisfaction as you finish up your working years or hand off to someone else. If you can't say that, the good news is, you probably have time to reconcile it. Professionally speaking, my clients at stage eight find satisfaction choosing and training their successor, so they leave their workplace in good shape. Others write their memoir or spend time focused on their children and grandchildren.

My mother worked right up until a few months before she died at the age of seventy-two. While I cared for her in her final months, I watched her peck away on her keyboard each day as she wrote out what she'd learned and wanted to pass on to future generations.[24] At her final birthday party, she was surrounded by her siblings, kids, grandkids, nieces, and nephews. We each hugged her as she whispered in our ears. Though cancer took her sooner than we'd hoped, she lived a full life and left her mark. At her memorial service, scores of colleagues spoke of her influence and passion, and I was proud to call this woman my mother. She was far from perfect, but she worked on her issues in her latter years. That's what made me so proud. This is what stage eight is all about—integrity.

Stage Eight Key Questions

1. How has my life mattered?

2. As I enter my latter years, how can I give back some of what I've gained?

3. What did I not accomplish that I wish I had? How has that provided a healthy humility as I enter my last season of life?

4. What do I still have time to put right?

EMBRACE YOUR STAGE WITH HUMILITY

Don't wish yourself out of the stage you are in. As hard as you try, you can't imagine yourself into the future before you're there. Living in the present will help you focus your attention on the immediate challenges.

Humility is an important part of your stage. The Latin origin of the word humility is "humus," which means "of the earth." A better recognized saying is, "salt of the earth." Someone who identifies with everyone. At its core, humility is an act of selflessness. Think on the implications of this.

You are aging and will die one day—dust returning to dust. Concentrate on enjoying where you're at; don't take it for granted. You've got valuable people in your life and critical work to do in this world. If you engage your stage with serious specificity, there is a much better chance of you finding peace when you lay your head down tonight and forever.

HOW THESE STAGES HAVE HELPED ME

My upbringing necessitated that I act as an adult before I was ready. Because my parents worked long hours, I was driving by the time I was fourteen. Though at the time I loved this independence, looking back on it, I wish I had more time to be a kid.

As I mentioned earlier, this freedom also landed me in a fair bit of trouble. As my high school years passed by ("in a puff of smoke"), I learned to put up a front to appear more confident than I really was. Ultimately, this landed me in charge of almost everything in my life. I gained leadership positions and well-paying contracts eventually. Problem was, I'd not learned to engage relationships without an agenda. Sure, I had a few close friends, but the people I could point to that I truly trusted were few. This eventually led to a mental breakdown at the age of thirty-seven.[25]

During that difficult time, I started getting lost and forgetting things. I encountered new pains in my hands and stomach that I still manage today. My heart felt unstable, and feelings of anxiety led me to believe I was about to have a heart attack. Why? I had not developed appropriately in the earlier stages, so my stage six relationships couldn't bear the weight of my brokenness. I felt alone. And though my mind checked out, my body sent me signals that I couldn't ignore.[26] This is how we decided to leave our home in California and move to the quiet of east Tennessee. Years of counseling helped me see how much I found purpose in helping everyone but myself. I needed to learn to face my past, get a healthier marriage, and find friendships with no agenda.

I look back on that time and see how blind I was. I was a productivity machine and found value in what I did. The problem was, this wore me out and alienated others— most importantly, my family.

Facing my past has helped me think more clearly about who I am and what I want to leave behind. Now that I'm a bit into stage seven, I realize as I write that I'm just a short time away from my kids leaving home, which will lend to a new phase in life. That's sobering and I want to take it seriously. Since my kids are older now, this has freed up some time to work on my marriage and gain clarity on my work as an author, speaker, and consultant. What will be the theme of my next season of life?

Knowing what stage I'm at has made all the difference. It's helped me find personal and professional focus. That's my hope for you, too.

Here's a synopsis of stages six through eight:

Stage	Key Concern	To embrace what you don't know means to acknowledge that...	To gain stability means...	Outcome
Six	Intimacy vs. isolation	You may not know how to engage relationships with trust and vulnerability. This will cause the rest of your life to break down. How can you start facing this?	Being surrounded by those you love, and who love you (with no agenda)	Learning to love
Seven	Generativity vs. stagnation	You may not have thought seriously yet about what you'll leave behind and the health of your family. This will leave you feeling empty and will make you uninspiring to follow. What would it mean for you to get serious about what's important to leave behind?	Meaningful work and a thriving family that's set up to contribute to the world when you're gone	Caring for others
Eight	Ego integrity vs. despair	You may have only focused on your work and neglected your important relationships. How can you use your latter years to put things right?	Peace with what you've done and happy with your relational legacy	Growing in wisdom

SUMMARY

Embrace what you don't know

Your life stage determines what internal tension you'll feel and what questions you'll ask.

Get humble by asking the right questions

What stage are you at? How does that impact where you currently need to focus? How has focusing on the wrong stage potentially derailed you from what's in front of you?

Get paid

Gain age-appropriate virtue that will enable you to serve the right group of people with integrity and peace.

APPLICATION

What chapter points do I need to remember right now?

....

....

....

....

....

....

....

....

How do I want to make movement in these areas?

....

....

....

....

....

....

When will I do it?

....

....

....

....

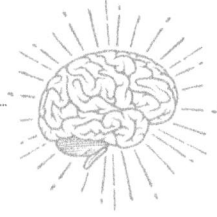

"When we accept ourselves for what we are, we decrease our hunger for power or the acceptance of others because our self-intimacy reinforces our inner sense of security."
—Brennan Manning

Chapter 2

CREATING STABILITY IN LEADERSHIP

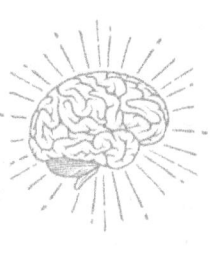

All right, it's time to put this book down and go ask your closest colleagues three questions. Do not ask these to your direct reports (they will most likely not answer honestly):

1. What do you see as my greatest strength?

2. How does overusing my strength potentially cost us?

3. What's a blind spot most people won't tell me about?

What did you learn? If you'd like to remember it, scribble it here: ....

I can almost guarantee that what you just learned is somehow related to your leadership outlook or focus. This chapter will explore how creating stability in leadership is intimately connected to you knowing these things about yourself and your team.

You're naturally wired with a certain set of strengths, potential blind spots, and a life stage that influences how you operate. To embrace what you don't know in leadership means having the courage to get help looking into your blind spots. By nature, a blind spot isn't seen. Asking for an outside perspective (like you just did) is essential. To illustrate, I'd like to tell you Kelly's story.

THE STORY OF THE EMOTIONAL MANAGER

Kelly was a talented leader working for a large water treatment company. She chose to step away from her role as a manager after giving birth to a wonderful baby girl. But after 15 months off, she returned to a very different work environment. In her absence, the organization had grown, changed, and there were different players at the table. Add to that, after six months back on the job, she also realized that *she* had changed.

Kelly was more emotional, appeared to lack confidence, and sometimes cried during tense meetings with her manager, who often used fear as a motivator. Kelly knew she needed help, so she approached her HR leader and asked for an outside perspective. Together, they discussed what Kelly had been experiencing and decided to get Kelly some coaching.

In our first sessions, I learned that Kelly was wired as a task-oriented leader. But since returning to work, she felt new feelings and was often overwhelmed and unable to speak up. "It's like I've lost my voice," she said. Prior to her leave of absence, she led from the front and was a hard driving manager. Kelly wondered what had happened.

"What's different now?" I asked one day.

"Having a child has changed my outlook on the world. I can't work the hours I used to, and I don't want to anymore, either. I need to be more intentional with family time and live a more balanced life," she said.

Kelly's life stage impacted the way she was feeling, thinking, and leading. Kelly (in her late 30s at the time) intuitively realized that though she'd been driving hard on her career earlier in her life, a shift was needed. But something was holding her back.

With the addition of a new baby, she saw the importance of developing deeper trust with her husband at home, with her team at work, and she needed to learn new ways to bear more emotional weight in those tense meetings. She seemed like a sponge that absorbed the negative emotional energy of those around. That weight was crushing to her personally, and I encouraged her to seek the help of a counselor to explore this subject more. I'm happy to say, that as she pursued counseling in this area, she found focus and freedom to think about the shifts she needed to make in her leadership.

As our sessions progressed, Kelly realized she needed to learn how to empower and support her team, not just tell them what tasks needed to be done. Also, she started learning to feel her emotions, find her thoughts, and discover her voice.

"What do you think is at the core of finding your voice?" I asked during one session.

"I think it has something to do with calling out what no one else is saying," Kelly replied.

"What's not being said right now?" I asked. At that moment, something clicked, and Kelly began to process a thought verbally.

"Maybe finding my voice is about learning to speak to the unspoken things?" Kelly went silent for a moment. "Wow," she said, and started writing this new idea down.

That was the beginning of Kelly using her voice. Soon after, she began speaking up in meetings, she learned to build trust with her team through regular one-on-ones and learned to empower them with clear and impactful feedback about their development. How did it begin? She faced her blind spots, sought feedback on what she'd been missing and, in her case, gained a reputation again for being a healthy and stable leader. As Kelly did this for herself, she was able to do it for others, too.

Kelly is currently up for a promotion and recently received an award for her outstanding charity work within her company.

"What I find inspiring is that we have the knowledge and resources to put an end to the clean drinking water crisis within my lifetime," she said. "I want to teach my daughter from a young age how privileged we are, but also how important it is to find ways to incorporate service and giving into our lives at every stage."

As I interviewed her for this book, Kelly told me, "I feel like I've found a higher cause to give my life to." (We'll unpack this idea more in the next chapter.)

The interesting thing about Kelly is that, though she needed to shift her way of leading, what was holding her back was the personal work she needed to do. Kelly's story illustrates how knowing your life stage impacts leadership. But it also shows the importance of knowing your leadership orientation and when the time is right to embrace a shift into a way of leading that you may not yet know. In Kelly's case, she needed to shift from being a task-focused leader to a people-oriented one.

Kelly got humble, asked the right questions, and got paid. But the payment I'm talking about is bigger than money. In Kelly's case, she got paid with peace and purpose. Now she turns her work off at night and enjoys her family. Add to that, when she's at work now, she's impacting the organization as a dependable people developer, and she's doing her part to make the world better. Kelly, if you're reading, you inspire me!

Healthy leaders (like Kelly) in stage six will often shift from task accomplishment to people development. Those in stage seven will sometimes shift from people development to creating purposeful work in the world. Kelly is ahead of the game, and that's all right. Whatever stage you find yourself, having a team of diverse members (age, ethnic background, and life stage) will broaden your human perspective and help expand your reach—as a person and as a company.

The rest of this chapter about facing the blind spots that may be preventing you from bringing stability in your leadership and on your team. Stability in leadership means that you know your orientation (life stage, personality, strengths, and potential blind spots) and how to get results through your team (who also knows the same). But before we learn the "hows," let's first look at the "what."

A SIMPLE DEFINITION OF LEADERSHIP

What is leadership? It's pretty basic, actually. Though leadership is influence, and the "capacity to turn vision into reality,"[27] those ideas translate practically into the ability to accomplish something important through others. There are scores of great books on this subject that tell us *how* to do this. But at its core, leadership is about the strategic movement from where you are to where you want to be (here to there) and achieving transformation in others along the way.

Good leadership creates stability, but there are often two blind spots that create *instability*. First, people sometimes have yet to recognize their leadership orientation (suffering from a lack of self-awareness). Second, they run short on real results because they don't know how to inspire their team to overcome challenges and move past mistakes. The following portion of this chapter is split into two parts: one for leadership orientation (which is about outlook and focus), and the other for getting results via teamwork.

PART ONE: LEADERSHIP ORIENTATION

If you don't yet know your leadership orientation, you're probably suffering from some blind spots (as your colleagues probably just shared with you). In an attempt to be respectful (to you, and to also not appear stupid), most people on your team will never say anything—pro or con—regarding your methods. However, if you open the door for critique and embrace what you may not know, you can learn how to improve your delivery and continue to hone your skills.

The good news is that you don't have to be great at everything—that's why you've got a team. Lean into their specific areas of strength for help. We'll talk more about that in a moment.

In terms of knowing your orientation, let's unpack two basic categories: outlook and focus.

Your Outlook

Remember that leadership is simply getting from A to B (here to there). Whether you think more about A or B reveals your primary outlook. Do you prefer tracking current progress and data? You're looking here (A). Do you often look farther out and dream up new plans? You're looking there (B).

Blind spots occur in leadership when you pay attention to one at the expense of the other. Good leadership has an outlook for here *and* there and makes a good plan for closing the gap in-between.

Two Examples: Where You Look

"HERE" OUTLOOK: Once, the CEO of a health care organization approached me to see if I'd work with a member of his executive team. We'll call him Matt. Matt was likable and a creative thinker, but he missed meetings regularly, wasn't hitting his objectives, and would soon be demoted if he didn't clean up his act (which I didn't know at the time). I did a series of interviews regarding Matt and learned that he rarely returned coworkers' emails or phone calls. When I inquired about this, Matt simply said, "I just have too much work to do."

Through coaching, we learned that Matt was living in reactive mode. He tried to address every interruption, and often forgot about team meetings he needed to be a part of. He was so focused on where he was at the time, that he lost sight of where he needed to be. The opposite scenario can be true as well.

"THERE" OUTLOOK: Years ago, I spent time working in a worldwide company that grew primarily through acquisitions. The CEO was known as a cowboy type who made major deals. He was hyper focused on numbers, and this worked well for investors. However, internally, things were a mess. Their teams were unhealthy and angry. Day to day tasks seemed to pile up at lower levels, and grown men with PhDs would tell me privately through tears how they hated their lives. This CEO knew where he wanted to go, and he got there financially. But he didn't pay attention to where he was at. Staff turnover was high, and lives were harmed. Eventually, that company was acquired by another. I hope that the culture within it is healthier now.

Your Focus

How will you pull off your plans? It's natural for goal-driven people to lean harder on tasks. Do you think up detailed strategies and genuinely believe an air-tight plan will get the job done? You're a task-focused leader. On the other hand, would you prefer to talk it over, brain-storm with your team, and address behavioral issues along the way? If that's the case, you're a people-focused leader.

A major leadership mistake is relying too much on the task at the expense of the people accomplishing or not accomplishing those tasks. Or it's the other way around, just as incomplete and inadequate as the first. Here are a few examples that illustrate the importance of a well-rounded style.

Two Examples: How You Focus

TASK FOCUS: I was called to work with a group of engineers and scientists who couldn't get along. These men were brilliant and logical thinkers, but socially tone deaf. It was normal to be snappy and sarcastic in that organization whenever a question was asked. "I shouldn't have to tell you that; that's why we hired you!" was a normal response.

I would follow up that reply with, "How would that response work in your marriage?"

"It wouldn't," one man answered. "Maybe that's why my marriage didn't work!"

The place erupted in awkward laughter, and multiple voices chimed in, "Same for me!"

Sad, I know. But in their brash braininess, they had lost their humanity. "If your marriage failed with that behavior, what makes you think your teams will succeed with the same behavior?" I stated. Things went silent as that idea got through to them. Over-focusing on tasks can eventually lead to a breakdown if unhealthy social interactions are ignored.

PEOPLE FOCUS: In another instance, I worked with the team of a faith-based non-profit that had a multi-million-dollar budget and a massive amount of influence. Their staff meetings spent copious amounts of time checking in with each other personally. But when it came time to track the actual work that needed to happen, missed commitments were minimized and people weren't held accountable.

When it came time to share feedback (some of it negative), it was suggested that we wait "just a little longer." The result was that the work didn't get done, and the lack of accountability eventually hurt people relationally. Over-focusing on relationship in a work environment can eventually lead to a breakdown of duties (and then relationship) if tasks are ignored.

Summary On Orientation

Is your outlook here or there? Is your focus on tasks or people? These answers make up your leadership orientation. Your team needs to know this so that they can better rally around you. They need to know their orientation as well. This means minding the tasks and the people factors (as you develop them).

Embrace what you don't know and invite your team to submit anonymous feedback about areas you can improve upon. Then get humble and ask them individually how you can better support them. The benefit you'll reap is knowing your own development needs and each person's needs on the team. Best of all, you'll have taken an important step in fostering a climate of growth.

PART TWO: GETTING RESULTS VIA TEAMWORK

If leadership is about getting from here to there, then getting results through a team is about guiding those individuals from present to future in the midst of daily work.

"The growth and development of people is the highest calling of leadership."[28] If you don't want to do that, then go be a one-person operation. Being a team leader necessitates helping the people on your team improve professionally *and* personally. If you can do this, you'll have a happy team.[29] Engaged teams are a byproduct born from their leaders' regular investment in their lives, clarity of communication regarding their contribution to the team's work, and regular feedback to let them know how they're each doing. This creates happiness, which leads to productivity. That equals high engagement.

The Main Obstacle

In order to understand team development, we must first see the main obstacle to team success. In our society, people get promoted through performance. That means if you've mastered a certain set of tasks, you progress up the ladder with license to tell others what to do. Let that sink in. You become a manager and leader of people based on your ability to accomplish tasks. See the disconnect?[30]

Would you put an expert psychologist—with the most amazing people skills—in an operating room to do brain surgery? Absolutely not. They would need to demonstrate a certain competency and have specific training to do that. Someone's life depends on it. Yet, in terms of leading people, it's a widespread corporate habit to put individuals without any people skills in charge of leading others.

Many times, solo-flying managers, who are great at communicating via concise office emails, find themselves freshly promoted and tossed into the strange waters of interpersonal team leadership. Suddenly, it's... *You mean I have to do the slow, mucky work of talking to other humans about what needs to be done? Give positive recognition? Hold someone accountable? Communicate the plan of action more than once and in person!?*

At this point, Mr. Miyagi (wise master in the *Karate Kid*) would say, "No such thing as bad student, only bad teacher." If the team is unhealthy, it's not their fault. It all comes back to the person in charge. However, if a leader is skilled in how to develop people—allocating and building their variety of strengths—they discover unparalleled productivity, thus driving personal engagement to its fullest potential.

How to Get Results Through a Team

Each person on your team needs to know two things at a minimum: (1) where the team is going and (2) what his or her individual part is. Since most conflict boils down to a lack of clarity regarding goals and roles, it's your job as the leader to clarify their direction at the beginning. This will determine the goals. After all, if we don't have a worthy cause to give ourselves to, then why are we even coming to work? Since we'll unpack this idea in the next chapter, for now, I want to focus more on individual team roles (and how to help them grow).

Considering the team or organizational goal(s), each team member needs to know their individual part in accomplishing the mission. The role of a leader is to ensure that along the way, each member knows their current state, and the desired state of growth. The leader's job is to track with each team member to ensure that they're developing on that journey, learning new competencies, and getting the work done. As they travel the path with you, you'll notice a certain kind of magic begins to happen. Communication becomes easier. Stress levels start to drop. Issues are resolved.

Owning Issues

When each team member is growing individually, they learn to own team challenges and organizational issues. John, the chief operating officer of a lumber company I work with, explained it rather well: "I often encounter people who want to get paid more. Then I ask them, 'Well, what issue do you want to own?' Sometimes they say, 'I don't want to own any issues, I just want a raise.' From there, I have to help them understand how promotion and compensation works."

At a training session I once conducted, John, who is near retirement, gave an insightful survey of corporate re-numeration over the last forty years.

"Up until the mid-90s, compensation was based on seniority," he said. "If you showed up and did a decent job, over time, you'd get paid more. But then things shifted towards performance, and it was a whole new ballgame. Suddenly, those who got paid more did so based on increased ownership of people and/or organizational issues."

What John was explaining to his managers was that it is easy to predict who is going to do well in a company based on how they step up to the plate to fix problems they see. And for those who are not so quick to take possession of concerns, regular development conversations can be the avenue to help address those matters needing to be owned.

Embracing what you don't know in leadership means inquiring into why your team may not be owning issues. When I was younger, I assumed the best in people and pretended everything was great (which was stupid). But I learned the hard way that smart leaders coach for regular improvement and have the courage to let team members go who can't (or don't want to) change. What I've outlined in the previous section, "How to Get Results Through a Team," is a pathway of how to do that. Your team will never know how to grow (or which issues to own) unless you create the environment for those conversations. This is how you get results through a team.

Kelly, from earlier in this chapter, needed a leadership shift as she matured. However, personal issues due to her life stage were holding her back. She embraced what she didn't know, inquired into her own life, and overcame those barriers. Additionally, in her leadership, she also embraced what she didn't know and worked with a coach, a mentor from within her company, and her HR leader to get help seeing into her blind spots. She needed to shift from a task manager to a people developer but didn't know how. From there, she got humble and asked the right questions. For her, that meant learning how to track regularly with the individuals on her team, have difficult conversations, and coach for growth. In the process, she discovered a Noble Cause to give her life to and is now getting paid with peace and purpose.

Don't you want this for yourself and your team? I do, and I want it for your organization. But before we unpack how to find a Noble Cause in the next chapter, let's encapsulate this chapter on leadership orientation.

Orientation	Key Concern	To embrace what you don't know means to acknowledge that...	To gain stability means...	Outcome
Here Outlook	Tracking current data, tactics, and meeting deadlines	You may lose sight of your strategic goals, and the team may lose sight of the "why" behind the work.	Asking your leaders to clarify the direction the organization is going. Out of that, create strategy meetings with your team so they see the big picture.	You and your team will see how small things add up to a big impact.
There Outlook	Thinking about and planning for the future	You may be neglecting details that could be making you inefficient.	Pulling together your detail-oriented teammates to ask their perspective on ways to make your work more efficient and impactful. Empower them to take ownership.	A data-oriented approach to meeting long-term goals.
Task Focus	Practical action items on my to do list	You may not give much thought to the people factors. 28% of employees cite poor communication as the reason they could not deliver on their tasks.[31]	Creating space to understand what people dynamics are preventing you from reaching your goals.	Better relationships and tasks that get done on time.
People Focus	Relational factors helping or hindering my team	You may be friendlier than you need to. Remind your team about the important work that needs to be done and hold them accountable to steady movement.	Regular tactical movement and improved relational satisfaction around teamwork.	Higher engagement and satisfaction

SUMMARY

Embrace what you don't know

Acknowledge your blind spots. Get teammates who shine to lend their abilities to the place you may not be looking (here or there), or where your focus is lacking (task or people). If you're not developing your team, begin meeting with each teammate regularly, and make sure they know their individual part in accomplishing the set goals. Discuss how they can improve. If you don't know how to do this, ask someone who is good at it, or hire an external coach to guide you.

Get humble by asking the right questions

Do you naturally look more here than there? Do you focus more on tasks or people? Does each member of your team know their development pathway and which issues they should own? What's holding you back from admitting your blind spots? How do you think acknowledging your blind spots would encourage your team members to recognize their own? How might that benefit your organization?

Get paid

Knowing your leadership orientation and how to get results through a team will help you excel at your high-priority tasks while improving your personal and working relationships. Depending on your organization, your team success most likely will lead to increased compensation for you and profit for your company.

APPLICATION

What chapter points do I need to remember right now?

How do I want to make movement in these areas?

When will I do it?

....

....

....

....

....

....

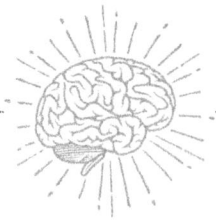

"The two most important days in life
are the day you are born and the day
you discover the reason why."

—Mark Twain

Chapter 3

CREATING STABILITY IN ORGANIZATIONS

How clear is your company on their reason for existing?

Some time ago, I worked with the executive team of a semi-conductor company. Before we started a strategy session, I always asked, "Why are we doing this?" In other words, what was the objective of the company—its Noble Cause? In this instance, here's what occurred.

"We exist to make money for our shareholders," one leader joked. Another added, "We make semi-conductors," while still another responded, "Our products support the military and GPS devices."

"Are you all right if we take some time to get aligned on the reasons we're creating this strategy?" I asked.

"Yes, this is an important conversation," the general manager replied. "Guys, we've got to be clear on this."

"All right," I said. "I'm away from my family for three days to be with you. When I get home, my kids are going to ask me what I did all week. If I tell them that I worked with a company that exists to make money for its shareholders, that won't mean anything to them. Explain why you exist in a way that would make sense to an eight-year-old."

A two-hour argument ensued. I listened and asked questions. We scribbled things on a flip chart. The tension in the room was palpable. I knew we needed to get this right.

"I think we exist to make the world safer," one person finally said. "If our products aren't right, people's GPSs won't work and even the military can't function correctly."

The room went still.

Almost in unison, everyone exclaimed, "That's it." They had found their Noble Cause.

The following day, I observed a strategy meeting where a discussion was taking place about whether or not to sell a specific product to another country. "We can't do that," the general manager said. "It won't make the world safer. And that's why we exist."

Today, this company still rallies around that Noble Cause. That moment was one of the proudest of my career. Knowing the reason for existing matters to the world. Are you clear on yours?

YOUR REASON FOR EXISTING

The Gallup Organization found that nearly 60% of employees don't know what their company stands for. "Since most organizations' purposes aren't clear," they explained, "it follows that their strategies and operating models are misaligned and unable to deliver optimal results."[32] Other research bears similar findings.

New York Times bestselling author and business lecturer, Dave Logan, Ph.D., found through over ten years of research that around 49% of organizations in the United States exist in a fragmented state where individuals within that company fight over who is great and who isn't. This creates a directionless culture that often goes toxic.

Shows like *The Office* are hard for me to watch because the comedy is so true. Yet, it makes sense why Michael Scott would say, "Sometimes I'll start a sentence and I don't even know where it's going. I just hope I find it along the way."[33] Unfortunately, Scott's metaphorical "sentence" is how so many businesses operate. As people show up for their daily work, leaders hope they'll find something along the way that motivates them to stay. It doesn't have to be this way.

The post–COVID–19 worker shortage has shown us that people have a choice, and they'll go somewhere else if their current employer only offers money. Why risk one's health and peace when death was found to be so close? People need a reason to work. Viktor Frankl, a psychologist who survived the death camps of World War II said, a person "Who has a why to live for, can bear with almost any how."[34] So how do we help our organizations get clear on the "why" of our existence?

Logan's findings teach us that the way out of this fragmented state is the shift from individual goals and values to shared values and vision. He calls this vision, a Noble Cause, which is a history-changing vision. An organization with a Noble Cause isn't comparing itself to anyone else because its main concern is global impact.[35]

These organizations know that making money is an indicator of success but doesn't always equate total success. After all, I could be a drug dealer and make plenty of money while destroying families and communities. Companies with a Noble Cause know that when money making is the ultimate goal, people will do crazy things to get there. However, when a company is clear on the reason they exist, they find healthy boundaries to operate within, and awe-inspiring things can happen. How clear are you on your organization's reason for existing?

Embrace what you don't know, and start asking why you exist and what you're hoping to accomplish that's worth doing in this world. In a company where the vision isn't clear, asking around may make you feel stupid, but as Confucius said, *"The man who asks a question is a fool for a minute, the man who does not ask is a fool for life."*

TWO ORGANIZATIONS WITH VISION

When stakeholders in your company know their Noble Cause and are motivated every day to work toward that vision, not only do people find a reason to live, but the world gets the benefit.

I'd like to tell you the stories of two men who found their Noble Cause, and then share how you can find yours, too.

LIVE FOR SELF OR SERVE THE POOR?

Millard was a successful lawyer and businessman and was a millionaire by the age of twenty-nine. Problem was, he was never around, and his wife was miserable. They had all the money they'd ever need, along with a boat, nice cars, and a lakeside cabin. Still, it wasn't enough to satisfy. Millard's wife Linda had an affair, threatened divorce, and left him. He found her in another city and the two of them did some serious soul searching. What emerged from those difficult times were two people who wanted to live for something bigger than themselves. They went deeper in their faith and traveled to other parts of the world to learn from others who were devoted to a life of service. As their vision crystalized, Millard and Linda Fuller decided to give away their wealth and dedicate their lives to provide affordable housing for the poor. [36] In 1976, they founded Habitat for Humanity—an organization whose Noble Cause has helped millions of people over the years.

Today, the vision of Habitat for Humanity is *To Build a World Where Everyone Has a Decent Place to Live.*

The Fullers' vision motivates thousands of volunteers every year, and Millard's heart still shines through. One *New York Times* article captured it well. After Hurricane Katrina, Habitat for Humanity built a house for a family who'd lost everything. Thinking about the children, Fuller wondered what they'd become. "We don't know, he said, "but we know one thing: if we give them a good place to live, they've got a better chance." [37]

Millard and Linda Fuller's story illustrates how finding organizational vision starts in the heart and soul of a person and grows from there. "Your vision will become clear only when you can look into your own heart," said Carl Jung. "Who looks outside, dreams; who looks inside, awakes." We've seen how this can work in a non-profit setting. But can it work in a for-profit business? Yes, it can. Here's Yvon's story.

CLIMB ROCKS OR SAVE THE PLANET?

Yvon loved to travel and climb rocks. Traveling the country in his 20s, it was a normal occurrence to sleep 200 days or more per year in his army-surplus sleeping bag beneath the night sky. Once, he was arrested in Arizona and spent over two weeks in jail on the charge of "wandering around aimlessly with no apparent means of support."[38]

Motivated to make better rock–climbing equipment, Yvon went to a junkyard one day, bought some tools, and taught himself blacksmithing. Shortly after, he began selling his products out of the trunk of his car. Yvon Chouinard wasn't a businessman, but he wanted to make a product that would last. What started as Chouinard Industries grew into what we know today as Patagonia.

As Patagonia grew in the late 1980s and the early 90s, a recession hit. They had to lay off their friends and colleagues, and it was heartbreaking. So Yvon took his leadership team to the mountains of Patagonia, in South America, to do some soul searching. "Why are we in business anyway?" he asked. They discussed how they wanted to make durable products and do mini-mal harm to the planet. The idea of helping the planet resonated with everyone in a new way. And that was the day, after nearly 35 years in business, something clicked. Yvon finally knew why he was in business.

Today, the vision of Patagonia is *To Build the best prod-uct, cause no unnecessary harm, use business to inspire and implement solutions to the environmental crisis.*

Patagonia gives away a portion of its profit to help environmental conservation, helped found the organic cotton movement, repairs over 40,000 of its garments a year, and encourages people to buy less. There's so much to tell about this company that has now influenced larger companies like Wal-Mart to be more environmentally conscious. I encourage you to get Chouinard's book, *Let My People Go Surfing*, to read the whole story.

What happens that inspires a man to give away millions of dollars a year? Why would people opt to have their old garment repaired vs. buy a new one? Why would larger companies call a relatively smaller one to inquire into Patagonia's unconventional business practices? It all comes down to a Noble Cause.

In September 2022, Chouinard surprised the world by putting Patagonia into a specially designed trust so all its profits can go to fight climate change and protect underdeveloped land around the planet. Now Patagonia's only shareholder is Planet Earth. Can you see how a Noble Cause changes things?

WORKING TOWARD YOUR NOBLE CAUSE

Maybe you're one of the lucky ones that came into this world crystal clear on what your life was going to be about. But if you're like me, you came into the world simply trying to survive. Congratulations, you met your goal! But now what? It's the same with many companies. We got into business to provide for ourselves and our families. But now that our goal is clicking along, we wonder, *what else is there*? What follows are a few simple thoughts on how to gain clarity on your reason for existing (your why, what, and how).

An exercise that may provide clarity on your *why*, is to write your own obituary. What would you like to be said about you when you're gone? You probably have more control over your life than you think. So go ahead, write your future in the form of what would be said about you when you're dead. This isn't morbid; it's actually quite visionary. What you write may give clues as to your personal "why" for existing.

A way you can find your "what" that you want to do in this world is to imagine you're very old. You sit on a park bench and your grandchild asks, "Grandma (or grandpa), what are you most proud of about your life?" What would you answer? I encourage you to do this exercise right now and see what comes up.

A last exercise you may try to help you discover your "how" is to solicit the help of a coach or counselor to dig into your story. Who do you wish you had when you were young? What needs went unmet in your life? How does this point to the kind of person and work you want to be and do in this world? What may come up for you are items connected to your values. These values will show you "how" you want to go about your important work in this world.

These exercises aren't exhaustive but are a simple way to start thinking about your Noble Cause. At its core, your vision is about a way you want to make this world better. A close friend of mine says that when we ask ourselves "why" about four or five times, then we get to our core reason for doing anything we think is important.

Embrace what you don't know and ask yourself what you *really* want to do in this world. Then ask yourself "why" a few times and see what comes up. Don't get caught wordsmithing any of this. Get all your thoughts out, be blunt, be rough. You can make it look and sound shiny later.

OBSTACLES

As you find clarity on your vision, the way you do business may need to change. Some people will want to stay, others will need to go. How you treat and develop people will morph into something new as well. Discovering what the new needs of your company are requires curiosity and a special kind of detective work.

A general rule of thumb: The more people that are on your team, the more organization that is needed. Having worked with companies as small as three employees all the way up to 30,000, I can tell you that the bigger the company, the bigger the demands on its leaders.

From my vantage point, I've seen how a business's willingness to change their behavior, plans and processes, dictates how small or large they will grow. Small or large isn't better or worse; it simply means that each organization will need to grapple with the scope of their vision and ask if their size helps or hinders that.

HOW TO CONTINUALLY IMPROVE

Companies usually approach me when they're experiencing a pain point. Sometimes it's in relation to low engagement survey scores. Their turnover is too high, people don't feel cared for or invested in, or any number of other issues. Other times, a less data-driven leader will say, "People here are miserable," and they have no idea why.

I recently spoke with the owner of a small emergency clinic. "We're making plenty of money," she said, "but I'm afraid that at some point, someone on our staff might commit suicide. The workload here is really stressful."

These pain points are a few examples of why I get contacted. Each one represents a different way I get to embrace what I don't know. I rarely know what to do right off, so I've got to get humble, ask the right questions (which I'll unpack shortly), and let it all simmer before I can design a program to help them improve, so they can carry out their important vision.

In your life, leadership, and organization, asking a few basic questions (then more and more) will glean for you a wealth of data to help guide you in the proper direction. And if you want to improve that, you'll work to change your worldview. What I mean is this: *You've got to believe you're missing something*. Once you make that mental shift, you'll be free to investigate, inquire, amass data, and most importantly—learn!

SIMPLE QUESTIONS

Have you ever seen those blurry pictures that when you stare at it for a while, an image rises off the page? That's called a stereogram. Most people can see the embedded image quickly with a little practice. The trick is that you've got to *lose focus* before you can find it. Nearly everyone loses patience when the image doesn't come into focus fast. Think of this when keeping up with organizational health. You've got to create a space to lose focus (forgetting your agenda) and stare at the blur until a clear picture emerges. This means asking a few basic questions to various individuals, contributors, and team(s).

1. What's working well around here?

2. What's not working?

3. What do you think could be done to fix what's not working?

4. What resources or training do you need to do your job better?

5. Is there anything else you'd like to say?

Depending on the company and its willingness to delve deep, I've asked these questions for a day, and I've asked these questions for a year. The longer I ask, the more clarity I get. I usually find key themes within six hours, and ideas to overcome the issues are usually already present within the company. Pairing general questions like this with industry-specific surveys can add important quantitative data to what you learn.

Once you find clarity on the issues, ask yourself how these issues may be hindering you from carrying out your vision.

ADDRESSING THE ISSUES: SLOW DOWN TO GO FAST

Big problems occur in organizations when you're moving too fast and get too afraid to slow down periodically to do a company health check. Whether it's your life, your leadership, or your organization, take time to do a similar exercise. It could be the very thing you need to go to the next level. Smart leadership isn't reactive and rushed. Instead, smart leadership knows that we can make most decisions better when we go slower and take an honest look at what's in our way.

The Forum Corporation found that when strategically fast companies "slowed down to speed up," they improved their top and bottom lines, averaging 40% higher sales and 52% higher operating profits over a three-year period. Ironically, when the slower companies tried to go fast without slowing down, it didn't work.[39] Something for you to mentally munch on.

SLOW DOWN TO GET DATA: EXAMPLE

I worked with a fast-growing property development company once that had high engagement and a positive team atmosphere, so the conversation was a surprise. "You're going to put up with crap everywhere," one team member said. "But if you've got friends..." she dissolved into tears. "Shared suffering has united us," another team member finished.

These teammates loved their CEO and would do anything for him. But as questions were asked and surveys were deployed, their obstacles came to the surface—from blurred and hidden to crystal clear. They didn't have the development processes to match their growing size. People worked in silos, and hiring was done reactively. This put core value-based team members in a tough spot because those hired in haste sometimes didn't represent company values.

This company decided to update its communication strategy and upgrade their training. In the years since, they have grown from three billion to nearly ten billion in transaction value.

Their Noble Cause (to provide superior customer service in the housing industry) was too important to keep moving fast. By slowing down, they took the time to remember who they were, where they were going, and address the obstacles in their way.

Your Noble Cause is important, too. Are you clear on it? Can you name the issues in your way?

Key Concern	To embrace what you don't know means to acknowledge that...	To gain stability means...	Outcome
Knowing and communicating my Noble Cause	Your people may not know the reason your company exists. You may not be clear either.	Asking yourself, and your team, "why did we get into this business?" Then ask why you do that a few more times. Once you get to the core, ask how that helps the world. This is your Noble Cause.	You, and your people, will find a reason to come to work. As Frankl said, "he who has a why can bear almost any how."
Addressing the issues that could stop us	You may be moving too fast and profit may have become the main goal. Profit is an indicator of success, but it's one indicator among many.	Asking the basic "what's working" and "what's not working" questions will help your people feel heard. It'll also give you data to know the types of issues that could be preventing you from achieving your vision.	You'll gain a roadmap to help you know how to develop your people and company culture so it can achieve your vision.

SUMMARY

Embrace what you don't know

Admit when you've not done the best job getting clear on your Noble Cause. Don't be afraid to slow down to amass hard data on how well you're doing as a company.

Get humble by asking the right questions

Have you done the slow work to get clear on your reason for existing? How can you uniquely make history? What is working and not working well in your organization? Often times perceived strengths are, in fact, weaknesses, and those who are perceived as weak have the answers to make you stronger. What would it look like for you to slow down and listen to those currently without a voice?

Get paid

Doing this work develops trust within your company or network. High trust organizations have high productivity, low turnover, and low confusion.[40] Oh, yes, and they get paid more!

APPLICATION

What chapter points do I need to remember right now?

....

....

....

....

....

....

How do I want to make movement in these areas?

....

....

....

....

....

....

....

....

When will I do it?

....

....

....

....

....

....

....

Conclusion

BRINGING IT ALL TOGETHER

Thanks for tracking with me this far. In this book, I've outlined how you can embrace what you don't know in your life, leadership, and in your organization. Growth starts when we can admit that we have blind spots and get humble enough to ask the right questions about what we may be missing. And if you embrace what you are apt to discover, you'll get paid by reaping its benefits.

Embrace what you don't know.

Get humble and ask the right questions.

Get paid.

That's it!

Embracing what you don't know in life means... learning what stage you're in while creating healthy relationships and work to match.

1. In life stage six, we learn trust and relationships.

2. Life stage seven is all about getting focused on your work and investing in your family.

3. Life stage eight and onward is about reflecting on your life and leaving the world better than you found it.

Embracing what you don't know in leadership means... knowing your orientation and how to get results through a team that owns issues.

1. Orientation is about where you naturally look (here or there outlook) and how you focus (task or people).

2. Getting results through team cooperation happens when we take individuals from here to there and help them learn the competencies needed to be their best selves. As we do that, they will learn to own issues, and the organization can't help but improve.

Embracing what you don't know in your organization means... being clear on your Noble Cause and overcoming the obstacles that could get in your way.

1. Your Noble Cause is your reason for existing; how you're going to make history.

2. Take the time to slow down, ask questions, and discover what's working well and what isn't. What ideas do people have about how to overcome the issues at hand? What resources do they need? Make space for them to add anything else they want to say.

As we finish this book, I want to talk about someone who embodies the principles I've written about. Remember Dr. Jones from the introduction? In this section, I'd like to share his story.

THE TALE OF THE STRUGGLING DOCTOR

I met Dr. Bill Jones (from the introduction) by coincidence. A member of my family had a medical need, and my wife ended up meeting him in his office. As they spoke, he learned about my work and asked if he could contact me. A few days later, we met over a coffee.

Dr. Jones shared how he grew up poor and had invested his entire life into his medical practice—building it from the ground up. With no retirement or savings and every dollar invested in the success of his clinic, he was worried and rightfully so.

"Where are you struggling most?" I asked.

Bill, not lacking in transparency, said, "As we grow in size, I'm finding I lack the skills to manage a team." That's when I knew I was with a man who was ready to embrace what he didn't know.

We ended up spending a few sessions discussing leadership and cooperative team building. He thanked me for "taking the time" to meet with him and said he would love to continue working with me. "I know you're really busy with bigger companies," he added almost apologetically.

"I'm not taking the time to meet with you," I said. "I'm *making* time to meet with you. The size of your business doesn't matter to me. I think you're a really interesting person and your story is compelling." Dr. Jones went silent with tears glistening in his eyes.

"No one has ever said anything like that to me before," he confided.

It touched me that a man—especially one of position and public respect—could be so vulnerable yet dignified. It made an impression.

Bill was asking important questions. How could he build a team? What was stopping him? What insecurities had him stuck? In turn, I questioned his questions. Why was it important that he build a team, right now? What held him back up to this point? What, from his story, made him behave in ways that were counterproductive to the health of his company? Questions like this enabled us to go deeper to understand his ways of operating in his life and leadership.

THE IMPORTANCE OF STORY

As our meetings continued, I learned more of Dr. Bill Jones's story. Like me, he'd grown up in a chaotic home. Like mine, his dad was drafted into the military, but instead of a deployment to Germany, he was sent to the Korean War. His mom grew up poor and tried to make a better life for her family (as my mother had), leaving home as a teenager. We identified on many levels.

As a kid, Bill was left alone for extended periods of time while his parents worked long hours. Once, at the tender age of eight, he rode the city bus sixteen miles to the nearest mall. His older brother was abusive, and Bill did anything he could to stay away from the house.

As an eleven-year-old, he rode his bike around the rural areas of Olympia, Washington, after school and into the evenings. This was 1983, by the way. The same year and area where the infamous Green River Serial Killer, Gary Ridgeway, preyed on young women.

His family moved away from Washington to a small town in East Tennessee where they reestablished themselves. It was a struggle for Bill to find peers he could identify with, but eventually he met his lifelong best friend, Perry. Bill finished grade school and eventually college in that same small town, paying his own tuition to become a doctor.

The years of school and residency took their toll. When Dr. Jones started his small medical practice, his marriage fell apart. In the divorce, he lost custody of his three children, his home, and nearly 400,000 dollars. With nothing left, he was forced to move into Perry's basement. Dr. Jones barely kept his medical practice but rebuilt it after this major financial setback. When I met him, he was on his second marriage, and it was struggling.

IN LIFE

I noticed that Dr. Jones didn't have a clear sense of identity. He was functioning out of an adolescent stage, focused on his aptitudes as a doctor and what he could achieve. He was good at his work, so that's where he put all his attention. However, that's exactly what led to the loss of his wife and kids. He was caught in an unhealthy cycle he was unaware of.

He longed to change but didn't know how. Through our sessions and his own personal work, Dr. Jones learned how to navigate relationships in a healthy way (stage six) and restored ties with his kids (stage seven). I'm sad to say that as he matured, he lost his marriage with his second wife. But he continued to work on himself and grow personally.

Now, years later, he has found meaning in life and work and has recently started dating an elementary school teacher.

IN LEADERSHIP

I did a little leadership coaching with Dr. Jones and helped him see that he was a "here"–focused leader who looked at tasks as the primary means of accomplishing his goals. The problem was, he took on too much at work, bypassed vacations, and grew intolerant and controlling of others when things didn't go his way. Through coaching with another member of my team, he learned that an aspect of a CEO's role is to model emotional and relational health to those around him.

Instead of being everything to everyone—poorly—he learned to depend on his managers to look beyond the urgency of the moment. He began to work on what was important for today as well as the outcomes he wanted for the future. In this way, he has continued to grow immensely as a leader.

IN HIS ORGANIZATION

When the Covid–19 pandemic hit, my normal work and travel stopped. I approached Dr. Jones to see if he was still interested in the organizational health assessment he had initially inquired about years earlier.

"I intended for us to work on that in the beginning. Instead, you gave me a new purpose and changed my life. I think now is the perfect time to work on the practice assessment."

After a few days of interviews, I learned that his employees didn't understand the intricacies of personality or teams. And his managers didn't know how to develop their teammates or hold them accountable through processes of regular feedback. Each member wasn't being true to their value, and everyone worked in a silo where backstabbing was normal. The office was dysfunctional—somewhat ordinary for many offices.

I launched a four-month long development program, and their workplace drastically improved. I've done other assessments and programs in his company since, and things continue to get better.

Five years ago, Dr. Jones's medical practice made $1.6 million in gross revenue. Since our work together, his revenue has grown to $3.8 million in 2022. He ended up needing to double the employees, quadrupled his doctor team, and his engagement scores are strong. People that work with him love him, care about him, and sacrifice daily for their company's Noble Cause—which is to provide compassionate and advanced veterinary care for all they serve.

Dr. Bill Jones is our family's veterinarian and loving care-giver to our dog, Ace. Bill has become a close, personal friend of mine. In fact, he's the one who encouraged me to write this book.

Embracing what you don't know matters. Bill did it and got paid, but in more ways than one.

Bill, I dedicate this book to you. You're an inspiration to me, and your work in our community matters. You are changing the lives of your employees, patients, and neighbors. You're becoming the man you always were. One worth following.

Thank you for inviting me in. I'm honored.

ACKNOWLEDGEMENT

A wise leader once said that students are not greater than their teacher. But the student who is fully trained will become like the teacher. With that in mind, I want to acknowledge and honor the man I learned from. Though I am the culmination of many friends and mentors, my friendship with Sam McKee was the catalyst that brought me into the world of leadership development. No other man on the planet shares so many similarities with me in personality and story. Sam, I love you like a brother and hope we will continue to make a difference in the world together until we are old men. Thank you for your investment in me.

ENDNOTES

1   https://www.child-encyclopedia.com/stress-and-pregnancy-prenatal-and-perinatal/according-experts/effects-prenatal-stress-child

2   Allender, Dr. Dan B. & Loerzel, Cathy. Redeeming Heartache: How Past Suffering Reveals Our True Calling. Grand Rapids, Zondervan, 2021. p. 236

3   https://www.inc.com/peter-economy/this-study-of-300000-businesspeople-revealed-top-10-leader-traits-for-success.html

4   https://www.drucker.institute/thedx/youre-no-leader-at-least-not-without-practice/

5   https://www.moyramackie.com/leadership-fears-imposter-syndrome/

6   Schein, Edgar H., Humble Consulting, How to Provide Real Help Fast. Oakland, Berrett-Koehler Publishers, 2016. p. 193.

7   https://www.history.com/news/how-the-challenger-disaster-changed-nasa

8   https://www.nbcnews.com/id/wbna10995817

9   Numerous surveys have confirmed a typical manager can spend 20% or more of his or her time on conflict (Thomas and Schmidt, 1976; Watson and Hoffman, 1996; Center for Creative Leadership, 2003).

10   https://www.mediationworks.com/conflict-cost-calculator/

11   https://www.cdc.gov/violenceprevention/aces/fastfact.html

12   https://culturesync.net/how-to-develop-your-noble-obsession/

13   https://www.history.com/speeches/nixon-i-am-not-a-crookgoo

14   https://www.fraud-magazine.com/article.aspx?id=4294987208

15   https://www.cnn.com/videos/us/2022/05/29/nra-board-member-uvalde-acostanr-vpx.cnn/video/playlists/top-news-videos/

16   https://hbr.org/2008/07/leaders-in-denial

17   Dodd, Chip, Ph.D. The Voice of the Heart: A Call to Full Living (Second Edition). Nashville, Sage Hill Resources, 2014. p. 116

18   https://brenebrown.com/podcast/brene-on-shame-and-accountability/

19   Thomson, Curt, M.D. Anatomy of the Soul: Surprising Connections Between Neuroscience and Spiritual Practices That Can Transform Your Life and Relationships. Carrolton, Tyndale, 2010. From the Introduction, p. XIV

20   Voice of the Heart, pp. 118-119

21   These stages were taken and adapted from https://en.wikipedia.org/wiki/Erikson%27s_stages_of_psychosocial_development (May 31, 2022)

22   For more information, see "The Wheel of Functioning" at https://sagehill.co/the-wheel-of-functioning/

23   https://blog.ted.com/vulnerability-is-the-birthplace-of-innovation-creativity-and-change-brene-brown-at-ted2012/

24   This time of life impacted me greatly. I wrote a book about it called In The Caverns: The Darkness of Grief and the Dawn of Life Change.

25   My mental breakdown was connected to giving care to my mother while she died (mentioned in the earlier footnote). Months of sleepless nights while trying to run a business and the disconnection from my family were important factors that escalated my unhealth.

26   For more information on this important subject, see: The Body Keeps the Score: Brain, Mind, and Body in the Healing of Trauma by Bessel Van Der Kolk, M.D.

27   https://www.forbes.com/sites/kevinkruse/2013/04/09/what-is-leadership/?sh=a2ed4b5b90ce

28   This is a quote from Harvey Firestone. I saw it while working within the Bridgestone/Firestone corporation with my colleague Sam McKee (whom I mentioned in the Preface). I've partnered with his organization, Evergreen Leadership, for over ten years. See http://evergreenleader.com/

29   https://www.tlnt.com/is-happiness-the-secret-to-engagement/

30   I learned this from a conversation I had with Professor Edgar Schein on December 18th, 2013, organized by my certifying institution, The College of Executive Coaching. Schein unpacks this idea in his book, Humble Inquiry: The Gentle Art of Asking Instead of Telling.

31   For companies with 100 employees, it's estimated that miscommunication costs $420,000 yearly. Communication barriers could be costing businesses around 37 billion annually. https://www.expertmarket.com/phone-systems/workplace-communication-statistics

32   https://www.gallup.com/workplace/310562/organizational-effectiveness.aspx

33   The Office, Season 5, "The Duel"

34   Viktor Frankl's book Man's Search for Meaning details his experience surviving the Holocaust and is a worthwhile investment of time for anyone looking to probe deep questions on what makes life worth living.

35   See more at Dave Logan's Ted Talk on this subject at https://www.ted.com/talks/david_logan_tribal_leadership/transcript?language=en, Logan's New York Time's bestselling book, Tribal Leadership, also covers this subject in detail. He found that only 2% of organizations in the United States have a "history changing" vision.

36   Bettie B. Youngs shares the Fullers' story in detail in her book, The House That Love Built (2007)

37   https://www.nytimes.com/2009/02/04/us/04fuller.html

38   https://bthechange.com/the-patagonia-adventure-yvon-chouinards-stubborn-desire-to-redefine-business-f60f7ab8dd60

39   https://hbr.org/2010/05/need-speed-slow-down

40   Lencioni, Patrick. The Advantage: Why Organizational Health Trumps Everything Else In Business. San Francisco, Jossey-Bass, 2012. p. 6

WHAT'S NEXT?

The Achata Coaching & Leadership Group was founded in 2011. Our Noble Cause is to make space for leaders to find vision. We do this through...

1. Leadership Coaching and Executive Health

2. Team and Strategy Development

3. Organizational Health and Leadership Training Programs

We are privileged to partner with people like you. Please find us on Facebook and connect with us via our website: https://achatacoaching.com/connect/

Let us know how this book has benefited you!

ABOUT DAVID ACHATA

 David is an author, coach, trainer, facilitator, and speaker. He brings over twenty years of leadership experience to organizations, team development, and training. He has facilitated and spoken at a wide variety of training events and retreats.

David has worked in various capacities from high school teacher, to pastor, to organizational health consultant. It was in the environment of church leadership that he began to interact with numerous business leaders in the community such as hospital CEOs, presidents of non-profits, and more. This unique experience gives him a window of understanding into the fast-paced world of executive leadership.

As a result of this, Achata Coaching Inc. was founded in 2011 to make space for leaders to find a better vision. Since then, David has had the pleasure of serving top leaders from multi-billion-dollar companies, local entrepreneurs seeking ways to enhance their effectiveness, and has worked in industries such as health care, manufacturing, property development, semi-conductors, veterinarian services, lumber, tires, and aerial firefighting among others.

He holds a master's degree in Spiritual Development (M.Div.), and is an ICF Certified Executive Coach (PCC). David is well-versed in using the MBTI®, CPI 260®, the TKI® and TTI Success Insights® DISC colors. He is a Certified Mentor Coach through the College of Executive Coaching and is a Five Behaviors of a Cohesive Team™ Authorized Partner. He lives in the mountains of east Tennessee with his wife and two children where he enjoys trail running, mountain biking, and tinkering with his 1969 Mercury.

www.ingramcontent.com/pod-product-compliance
Lightning Source LLC
Chambersburg PA
CBHW082105140626
46553CB00018B/882